BANKING REFORM IN THE UNITED STATES

A SERIES OF PROPOSALS

INCLUDING A

CENTRAL BANK OF LIMITED SCOPE

BY

O. W. M. SPRAGUE

ASSISTANT PROFESSOR OF BANKING AND FINANCE
IN HARVARD UNIVERSITY

CAMBRIDGE
HARVARD UNIVERSITY
1911

NOTE

THE four articles in this volume were published in the Quarterly Journal of Economics for May 1909, February, August and November 1910. Only the first of them has been subjected to any very considerable revision. Matters which are considered more in detail in the subsequent papers have been omitted, corrections and additions have been made, and the tone rather than the substance has been modified. Convinced that a central bank patterned after those of Europe would not fit into our system, I drew the unqualified conclusion that a central bank would not prove a remedy for our financial ills. Further reflection led to the proposal of a central bank of limited scope which is brought forward in the final chapter. Without much change in substance the phraseology of the first paper has been modified in many places so as to make evident that its arguments apply only to central banks of the European type exercising influence primarily through their lending operations and discount policy.

HARVARD UNIVERSITY,
December, 1910.

CONTENTS

CHAPTER I

CRITICISM OF PLANS FOR A CENTRAL BANK OF THE EUROPEAN TYPE

CHAPTER II

PROPOSALS FOR STRENGTHENING THE EXISTING BANKS

CHAPTER III

PROPOSALS FOR STRENGTHENING THE EXISTING BANKS
(Concluded)

CHAPTER IV

A Central Bank of Limited Scope

BANKING REFORM IN THE UNITED STATES

CHAPTER I

CRITICISM OF PLANS FOR A CENTRAL BANK OF THE EUROPEAN TYPE

During recent years, and especially since the crisis of 1907, the proposal to establish a central bank in the United States has received an increasing measure of favorable consideration, and is now being urged by an influential body of bankers and others interested in the improvement of our present system. Dissatisfaction with the working of our credit machinery has become general, and is certainly not without foundation. It is an exceptional year that does not witness troublesome friction in its operation, while on occasion of severe financial strain it has almost invariably broken down, with disastrous consequences to the entire business community. To establish a central bank as a remedy for these ills would indeed involve a radical and even revolutionary departure from our banking traditions and practice. But therein may perhaps be found no small part of the attractiveness and promise of the proposal. Legislative safeguards are already far more numerous and detailed than in any other country, and our banks hold more money in proportion to credit liabilities than is customary elsewhere, with the possible exception of France. In spite of these apparent sources of strength, fluctuations in the rates for loans in our financial centers are far more violent than in London and other European capitals. This, however, is a small matter compared with the successive suspensions of cash payments to which our banks have resorted during the three great crises which have taken place since the organization of the national banking system.

Observation of the superior results achieved elsewhere certainly affords a most humiliating contrast, an apparent explanation of which is the presence of a central bank in all the principal commercial countries, with the exception of the United States. In this connection it is noteworthy that the main causes to which our troubles are commonly attributed are found in our peculiar methods of dealing with matters which are elsewhere made the concern of central banks. The withdrawal of money from general use under the operation of the independent Treasury system is unknown where central banks are employed as government fiscal agents. A more or less elastic note issue is secured in all countries having central banks, with the exception of England. Finally, these banks are the main stay of credit in times of acute financial strain. Conservatively managed, as they commonly have been, they have been able to lend freely in emergencies, and have also taken the lead in securing united action among the other banks. Certainly, foreign experience seems to warrant the belief that a central bank might prove an adequate remedy for our financial ills.

To these considerations in favor of a central bank, additional force is given when recent foreign literature and legislation on banking are considered. In his classical work upon the proper policy for a central bank, Bagehot, writing nearly forty years ago, was not convinced that the monarchical principle in banking was by any means the best. He accepted it for England as a product of long historical growth familiar to every one, and therefore better than a more perfect system, which would require revolutionary changes. But since his day the central banks have become stronger and more conspicuous; new ones have been established, notably in Japan and Switzerland; and without exception they have grown in power and prestige. This development, it is true, has not been due to banking causes alone. Political and also military considerations have been potent influences. But there can be no question that in European business circles, as well as among economists, the central bank has been generally accepted as a valuable, if not indispensable, feature in a highly developed and satisfactory banking system.

With so strong a presumption in its favor the proposal to establish a central bank of the European type [1] in the United States deserves thoughtful attention and careful analysis. Weighty objections to the plan must be based upon grounds which make it reasonably certain that the central bank could not achieve those results which have been secured in other countries. Certain difficulties, however, which

[1] It may be objected that there are wide differences between the various European central banks. This is indeed true, but there is uniformity in the two most fundamental matters, the holding of the ultimate reserve and the discount policy.

are not fundamental may properly be given at least passing attention. They are of a nature of which account must be taken if general public approval is to be secured for the measure, and which would render the task of a central bank exceptionally burdensome.

With the exception of Russia, there is no country of anything like the area of the United States in which we may study the operations of a central bank, and comparisons drawn from that country would be valueless, and even misleading, because of the relatively slight development of its credit machinery and on account of the autocratic power of the Russian government. Whether difficulties of a serious nature would manifest themselves on account of the size of the country must therefore be largely a matter of personal opinion, as to which wide differences may be expected. It may, however, be stated with some confidence that it would not be possible for a central bank to place a branch in every locality, taking, for example, the county as a unit. Thousands of branches would be required to provide facilities as generally accessible as those afforded through the five hundred branches of the Bank of France or of the Bank of Germany. Administrative difficulties would be insurmountable, to say nothing of the almost equally serious obstacle of a political nature arising from the bitter opposition of local bankers.

But numerous branches are not essential for the successful operation of a central bank. The Bank of England, which has but eleven branches, is in this matter a more suitable example. Branches in fifty or perhaps one hundred cities might be expected to

afford the means of extending the operations of the
central bank to all parts of the country. The control
of these branches would, indeed, be peculiarly difficult on account of the distances which would separate
many of them from the head office. Here the example
of Canada might be thought to supply a precedent.
But the situation is not exactly parallel, because
of the vastly greater responsibilities which would
rest upon the managers of the branches of a central
bank on account of the peculiar nature of its business.
Finally, an interesting minor consequence of the size
of the country may be noted. It would not be possible
to despatch money or notes from the head office to
the branches, or to other banks throughout the country,
between the close and the beginning of business hours
on successive days. It would be necessary to keep
a supply of funds at the various branches throughout
the country. Moreover, the requirements of the other
banks in making provision for abnormal withdrawals
of money by depositors would also be larger than
in other countries. The physical concentration of
reserve could not, therefore, be carried with safety
so far as in smaller countries, and a somewhat larger
reserve would be required in proportion to the total
demand liabilities of the banks of the country.

Closely connected with the size of the country is
the variety of its economic activities and the wide
differences in stages of development reached in its
different sections, especially in respect to the accumulation of capital. It would be extremely difficult
for the management of a central bank to analyze
correctly the business situation and to forecast the

immediate future, — matters which are essential to a determination of the proper discount policy to be adopted at any particular moment. In this respect, however, the situation would perhaps not be more complex than that which confronts the management of the Bank of England on account of the international position of the London money market. A more serious difficulty seems to be found in the distrust of, and even hostility towards, the Eastern financial centers, which still persists in those sections of the country which are primarily agricultural. This attitude is an inevitable consequence of the position in which the people of a newly settled region find themselves, when, in order to develop its resources rapidly, they have borrowed largely from distant capitalists. But the accumulation of capital, as well as the liquidation of debt, has been a notable feature in the recent economic history of the Western States, and already the traditional feeling towards the Eastern creditor has faded to a shadow of its former self. On the other hand, a less sectionalized but more diffused feeling against wealthy financiers has been created by the investigations and agitation of the last few years. The present juncture is an unfavorable moment for the establishment of a central bank, because men having the experience required for its management can hardly be found outside the circles of those who as a class have been the subject of wide-spread and exaggerated doubt and discredit. It is to be feared, especially if the Bank is to be one of imposing magnitude, that, in order to allay alarm from the two sources above mentioned, the details of organization would be prescribed and the powers of the management restricted in ways which might seriously impair its usefulness.

Were objections to a central bank solely of the kind which have been examined up to this point, it might be said with truth that every radical change must present difficulties as real and as serious. No one of the objections or all of them together could afford ground for the opinion that a central bank might not, at least in the course of time, give to our banking system those elements of strength and efficiency which it is agreed upon all hands are now sadly lacking. In the preceding paragraphs, however, we have by no means reached the heart of the problem. It is essential that we examine the particular powers and devices made use of by existing central banks in the exercise of their peculiar functions. Only after the effectiveness of these powers and devices in varying circumstances has been determined, will it be possible to form a reasonably accurate estimate of the results which may be expected from a central bank of the European type in the United States.

The special functions of central banks may be grouped under three heads: they serve as fiscal agents of government; they have large powers of control over the currency through the more or less complete monopoly of note issue; and, finally, since they hold a large part of the reserve of the other banks, they are directly responsible for the foundation of the entire structure of credit. This last is by far the most important function of central banks. Indeed, in a general but very true sense, central banks may

be said to have but this single function, — to insure
the maintenance and smooth working of the systems
of credit, of which they are the most important, tho
not necessarily the most considerable members. It
is a duty which rests upon central banks because
the other banks, which hold little or no cash reserves,
rely upon their deposits at the central bank and upon
the expectation of being able to borrow from it through
rediscounts or direct loans.[1]

This centralization of bank reserves has been everywhere a characteristic feature in the evolution of central banks. Historically, it is probable that it came
about in large measure as a result of the monopoly
of note issue and of the government business handled
by them. Such is quite certainly the case with the
Bank of England, the earliest central bank in date
and the model for all others of its kind. Through
its government business other banks were inevitably
brought into daily contact with it, and the convenience of an account upon its books became readily
apparent. Again, the right of note issue, in a period
when banking methods were undeveloped, was an
advantage which, along with its government business,
gave the Bank of England a position of unquestioned
superiority, both in size and in prestige. From
keeping a balance to keeping their entire reserve in
the central bank required no essential change in the
every-day methods of business of the other banks.
This stage had been reached in England before the
close of the eighteenth century, and for generations

---

[1] The London banks do not borrow directly from the Bank of England. They
withdraw money lent to bill brokers, who in turn are obliged to borrow from the Bank.
The difference is one of form rather than of substance.

English bankers have held in their own vaults only such amounts of money as are required for every-day purposes, — till money, as the English are wont to designate it. This custom was still further strengthened in 1854, when the plan was adopted, in the settlement of clearing balances, of simple transfers upon the books of the central institution. In other countries, virtually the same situation has been reached. Altho the other banks may hold a slightly greater amount of cash, they carry balances, larger or smaller, with the central bank, and are quite as dependent upon it to meet extraordinary requirements.

A somewhat analogous situation is familiar in this country. It was being developed before the Civil War from motives of business convenience, step by step with the more intimate commercial relations which improved transportation made possible between different sections of the country. Our national banking law crystallized this development at a point of somewhat less concentration than has been reached by European banks without legislative restrictions. With us any unusual demand for money sooner or later involves withdrawals from New York, not indeed from any single New York bank, but from some one of the ten or twelve banks in that city which hold practically all the deposits of outside banks. The situation of these banks, and in a minor degree that of the banks in other reserve cities, is similar to that of a European central bank, and the responsibilities incurred are of the same nature. A most striking difference is that the European central banks recognize this responsibility and understand the policy which they should adopt, while our reserve-holding banks do not. The responsibility is apparently so scattered that it is not sufficiently felt.[1] Here the establishment of a central bank would seem a hopeful means of improvement, since it is obviously more easy to secure effective action from a small number of closely associated directors of a single bank than from the directors of many banks, especially when they are not all in the same locality.

It may be seriously questioned whether it is either practicable or desirable that reserves should be concentrated in the United States to the extent customary in Europe. The deposit liabilities of the banks of the United States are more than twice as large as those in any other country. Moreover, on account of the size of the country and the number of its banks, an exceptionally large reserve is required for a given volume of deposits. With the complete concentration of reserves the amount of money and the extent of business of the central bank would become portentously large. It seems more practicable that the banks should continue to hold at least as great a portion of their reserves in their own vaults as is now customary. The burden upon the central bank would be somewhat diminished, but not to such an extent as to weaken the force of comparison with existing central banks. Our central bank would doubtless be relied upon to supply unusual requirements for money, the other banks in the absence of special

[1] The concentration of reserves in the United States is greater than is often supposed. Six New York banks (the City, Bank of Commerce, Park, Hanover, First, and Chase) hold three-fourths of the bankers' deposits secured by the New York banks, and there are scarcely fifty banks in all the reserve and central reserve cities with bankers' deposits of more than $5,000,000.

preventive provisions [1] regarding the reserve held by them as a sort of permanent foundation of credit, not as something to be used.

A much more difficult problem presents itself with regard to that proportion of the reserves of banks which is now deposited with banks in reserve and central reserve cities. At present the national banks in the three central reserve cities alone hold about $600,000,000 of net bankers' deposits, and the banks of the reserve cities hold about two-thirds as much more. Whether all, a part, or none of these deposits are to go to a central bank is a matter of the utmost importance. Doubtless, in any circumstance, a part of these deposits would be retained by their present holders. Consideration of business convenience and the probability that the central bank, following the custom of similar institutions in other countries, would not pay interest, would tend to the continuance, to a considerable extent, of existing arrangements. No great change seems to be expected by those who urge a central bank, tho this is, perhaps, owing to a failure to give the matter careful consideration. [2] Its fundamental significance will appear at a later stage in this discusson.

In the exercise of their function in relation to the reserve, the possession of government balances and the monopoly of note issue are valuable instruments

[1] Means of insuring the use of their reserves by the other banks is the most essential feature of the plan for a central bank brought forward in the final chapter. See pp. 158–162.

[2] It has been suggested that only the banks of central reserve cities should be permitted to deposit a part of their reserve with the central bank. See the address of President Geo. M. Reynolds before the 1909 convention of the American Bankers' Association. This proposal is considered briefly on p. 51. On the arrangements regarding deposited reserves in my own scheme, see pp. 95, and 162.

in making effective the means adopted by central
banks. But neither of these advantages, it should
be noted, is essential to the working of a central bank.
Government balances are at times so small as to be
of little service, and in the case of the Bank of England
the right of note issue is of no practical importance
whatever, since the Bank of England note is virtually
nothing more than a gold certificate. Even in countries where the central bank is able to extend its credit
in the form of notes, it is still true that the means
used in the furtherance of the reserve policy are,
in substance, similar to those of the Bank of England.
The right of note issue, as will be seen later, is simply
a valuable resource in the furtherance of a policy
which would be adopted in any case. This is a matter
which cannot be too strongly emphasized, since the
proposal to establish a central bank in the United
States is being urged by many primarily in order to
secure a mechanism for the issue of notes.

In analyzing the operations of a central bank, three
situations may be distinguished with regard to which,
tho the general purpose is the same, the policy adopted
is strikingly different. These three situations are:
first, periods of normal business activity; second,
periods of moderate financial strain; third, periods
of acute strain and panic. In the following pages
the activities of European central banks will be studied
in each of these situations, comparison being made
from time to time with what may be reasonably expected from a similar institution in the United States.

I

ACTIVITIES IN NORMAL TIMES

The activities of a central bank in normal times are of a comparatively simple and even routine nature, not very different from those of the other banks about it. In some countries on account of statutory requirements, and in all countries from motives of sound policy, its loans and other investments are confined to those which are deemed of high quality, a decided preference being given the trade bill over the collateral loan. The high quality of the assets is not, however, insisted upon with the intention of converting them into money in times of emergency. A central bank is then the refuge of last resort for the other banks, and any attempt to call in loans or realize on securities at such times would be directly opposed to the working principles of the central reserve banking system. It invariably happens at such times that the loans of central banks are largely increased.[1] The good quality of the assets in general is important because it gives that prestige which is half the battle for a central bank. A reputation for conservative, sound judgment is absolutely essential to the maintenance of universal faith in the strength of the central institution. For this reason, and even more in order to be able to meet the responsibilities of its position, it is equally essential that a central bank should hold a very large reserve against its credit liabilities. There is, of course, no precise

[1] There is, indeed, one kind of loan to which this statement does not apply, — the foreign bills held by many of the Continental central banks; but see p. 39.

proportion of reserve which is everywhere adequate amid varying circumstances. The general character of the economic activities of the country and the size of its entire credit structure must be the determining considerations for each central bank. In all countries with such institutions there has been a distinct tendency to maintain a larger reserve than was thought necessary twenty years ago. This seems to be due to a more clear recognition of their responsibilities, and because these responsibilities have increased with the growth of other banks and the more intimate relations between the markets of the world. After the Baring crisis in 1890 it was generally felt that the reserve of the Bank of England was too small. The proportion to deposit liabilities which, in normal times, had been in the neighborhood of 40 per cent, was therefore increased to rather more than 45 per cent. Even this proportion is now thought by many to be hardly sufficient. The Bank of Germany holds about the same proportion of reserves as does the Bank of England, and the reserve of the Bank of France, for many years, has been notably greater than that of any other country.

The ability to earn reasonably satisfactory dividends while maintaining these large reserves may well be given a word of explanation. Central banks do not pay interest upon deposits, and where, as in the case of the Bank of England, large deposits are received from the other banks, a basis for remunerative business is secured. In Germany, and especially in France, the right of note issue provides the money for the reserve at practically no expense to the central banks, since notes may be subsituted for money which would otherwise be required in every-day use.[1]

A highly important tho rather obvious consequence of the holding of large reserves should not be overlooked. Central banks do not in ordinary times make use of their entire lending power. They are a sort of reservoir of money and credit for use in emergencies. The other banks do lend to the full extent of their resources, and in the United States all of the banks follow that policy. The consequent absence of any reserve of lending power in the United States is a fundamental source of weakness in our system. Whether it can be best remedied through a central bank or in some other way is the central problem of this discussion.

In securing business, a central bank experiences no difficulty when the available funds of the other banks are regularly insufficient to meet the demand for loans. Until quite recent times this was generally the case, and is still the constant situation in Japan and Russia. This demand is everywhere highly irregular, and in Western Europe, while occasionally taxing the strength of the central banks, is often entirely absent. All central banks, therefore, compete with the other banks lending to individual borrowers. But in this competition, for reasons which will be noted later, they are at a great disadvantage and have been able to secure only a diminishing proportion of the growing volume of banking business of all

[1] An increase in the note issue of the Bank of England does not increase the banking reserve, because of the complete separation of the issue and banking departments since the Act of 1844. The Continental practice is followed in the plan presented in the final chapter, see p. 171.

kinds. The resources of the other banks have increased
to such an extent that, except when business is very
active, they are able to satisfy the entire demand
for loans. In England, France, and Germany there
are now banks which, measured either by loans or
deposits, are larger than the central banks of those
countries. This tendency has been most pronounced
in England, but only because of the more complete
development of its banking system. Between 1897
and 1908 the average deposits and the average reserve
of the Bank of England, while fluctuating not a little
from year to year, showed no appreciable growth,
being about £50,000,000 and £25,000,000, respec-
tively. During the same interval the deposits of
the other banks in the United Kingdom increased
from £720,000,000 to £850,000,000. The published
figures do not permit an exact comparison of the
growth of loans, but there is every reason to believe
that the showing would be no more satisfactory from
the point of view of the Bank of England. There
has therefore been a decided falling off in the proportion of its reserve to the total deposit liabilities
of all of the banks. The experience of the Reichsbank has not been more satisfactory, tho it has
the advantage of being able to strengthen its reserve
through the substitution of notes for coin in general
circulation. In 1897 its average reserve was £43,000,-
000, but it was hardly able to retain this amount
during the following ten years of irregular tho
generally active business. The rapid industrial development of Germany in recent years has been accompanied by at least equally rapid expansion of

credit by the other German banks.[1] Not even the
skilfully directed policy of the Reichsbank has been
able to strengthen the foundation of the credit structure.[2] The very considerable increase in the reserve
of the Reichsbank since 1907 is of no particular significance, since under any system, money commonly
accumulates in the banks at times of acute depression.
In France the reserve of the central bank has been
notably increased during the last few years, but,
it may be confidently asserted, not primarily or even
largely because of special influence of the Bank of
France. The industries of France change but little
from year to year, either in volume or in general
character. The accumulation of capital is extremely
large, and there is constantly a surplus seeking investment. In France, as in other countries, the influences
which in the long run determine its condition are
largely beyond the control of the central institution.

This failure of central banks to increase their operations to an extent sufficient to retain a permanent
proportion of the increasing total of banking business
requires some detailed explanation. In part it is
due to a relative increase in the kinds of business
which central banks are unwilling to accept. The
over-draft in particular has become to an increasing
extent a favorite method of borrowing in the European
business world. It has many of the advantages of

[1] W. Prion, Das deutsche Weschseldiskontgeschäft contains by far the best account
of the working of the German money market. For England, Bagehot's Lombard
Street is indispensable; but upon the working of the banking system at present the
reader should consult the admirable work which appeared in 1909, under the rather
misleading title of The Meaning of Money, by Hartley Withers.

[2] Had the German deposit banks been required to hold a cash reserve, the gold
holdings of the Reichsbank would have been enlarged, through the exchange of
gold for notes which would have taken place.

the demand loan, familiar in American banking. The borrower pays only for so much of the loan as he actually uses. In all countries purely domestic business dealings seem to give rise to a relatively diminishing volume of commercial paper in the form of bills of exchange, the kind of paper which central banks are most ready to take. During the greater part of normal years, moreover, the central banks are experiencing increasing difficulty in securing any part of the business of the very highest class. This is largely owing to the lack of flexibility in the terms upon which central banks are accustomed to accommodate borrowers. There are two official bank rates,— the rate of discount and a somewhat higher rate for collateral loans. The market rates (that is, the rates of other banks and brokers) are highly flexible, corresponding to every slight variation in the character of the security, the duration, and other conditions of the loan. The best paper is therefore ordinarily not brought to the central bank, tho in Continental countries, shortly before maturity, it is often rediscounted in order to take advantage of the admirable collection facilities which these institutions have provided. The Bank of England has frankly recognized this situation, and for many years has followed the market rates in dealings with regular customers. The Reichsbank adopted the same policy for a number of years, but discontinued it in 1896, largely on account of agrarian protests.

The suggestion has frequently been made that, if in normal times the official rates were reduced to a level with the market rates, no difficulty would be experienced in securing all the business which a central bank might care to take. But this would not serve the purpose, because market rates would almost certainly recede still further. This is because there are a number of long-established customs which give the official rates an indirect influence upon the market rates. In England and Germany, for example, the interest paid by the other banks upon time deposits, and the rates for certain kinds of loans,[1] fluctuate in a fixed relation to the official rate of discount. Even when the market is well supplied with funds, therefore, the market rates are seldom entirely uninfluenced by the official rate. But, if at such times the bank rates were further reduced, the market rates would almost certainly experience still further decline, and the effort of the central bank to secure additional business of the highest class would be unsuccessful.

The growth of the business of the other banks has tended to increase the fluctuations from week to week of the business of central banks in quite normal years. This is especially noticeable at the end of each quarter of the year. The various payments and transfers of credits and money which everywhere occur at those times make it necessary for the market to resort to the central bank. The requirements for these purposes may not have increased relatively to the total amount of banking business, but they have increased when measured by the growth of the business of central banks. During the last two

[1] In particular, rates on over-drafts and upon documentary foreign bills secured by perishable goods.

weeks of December in recent years of active business, the loans of the Bank of England have increased by upwards of £15,000,000, — an amount probably equal to half the loans of the Bank at other times. In Germany the same phenomenon may be observed, with this difference, — that in London deposit credits are sufficient for the purpose, while in Germany, owing to the slight use of checks, either specie or notes are required. To meet this requirement, provision was made in the act of 1909 for renewing the charter of the Reichsbank allowing a temporary expansion of its untaxed issue at the end of each quarter of the year. Requirements of this nature are quite normal, and are met without much difficulty, since they can be foreseen, and because the central banks do not use their entire resources at other times. On the other hand, they afford evidence that the growth of business of the other banks is placing an increasing burden upon the central banks.

In the United States the difficulties of a central bank from the causes mentioned above would probably be considerably greater than in any other country. It would experience great difficulty in procuring business of the highest class from individual borrowers because it would be obliged to enter into competition with powerful banks which already occupy the field. Moreover, it is to be expected that weekly and seasonal fluctuations in quite normal years would be far more violent than in any other country. The greater volume of credit transactions would by itself have this effect. Account must be taken also of the extent to which this is still primarily an agricultural

country, and its economic activities are of a highly
speculative and unstable nature.

An even more serious obstacle to the acquisition
of a volume of steady business lurks in the various
plans for a central bank which have been brought
forward. Altho the results expected are similar to
those achieved in Europe, these plans without exception include one important provision quite unlike anything found elsewhere. It is proposed to
establish a bankers' bank pure and simple, which
shall not be permitted to compete with existing banks
by making loans to individual borrowers. It is
evident that this restriction must greatly weaken
the force of analogies drawn from the working of
European central banks, at least in normal times.
Fluctuations in the volume of business secured by
the Bank would certainly be accentuated. In periods
of severe business depression there would probably be
no demand for accommodation whatever. As regards
the situation in years of normal business activity there
is more uncertainty, but consideration of this matter
may with advantage be deferred to a later stage in
this discussion.

After this outline of the normal activities of a
central bank, we are in position to consider in somewhat greater detail the minor functions of issuing
notes and acting as government fiscal agent. The
utility of central banks in the latter capacity is clear
and unquestioned. Public receipts and expenditures
are handled at little or no cost to the government,
and the money market is subjected to no serious

inconvenience. Even when revenue is largely in excess of expenditure, there is only that temporary tightening of money rates always incidental to the shifting of credits. The market rate of discount is advanced more nearly to, or even to a level with, the bank rate, and the central bank secures a larger portion of the total current business. The amount of government funds is, in the countries now having central banks, seldom large enough to impose great responsibilities or to create alarm at the power which an enormous surplus might give. The budgets of most countries are designed with an eye to equality of income and outgo, and only towards the close of the fiscal year, or after the issue of a war loan, are government deposits inconveniently large. In England, France, and Germany government balances are usually between twenty-five and fifty million dollars. During the last four years the maximum in France was $78,000,000 and in England $99,000,-000. In both countries the balance is kept from falling much below $20,000,000 by the issue of short-term government obligations. Finally, it should be observed that, as government fiscal operations follow much the same course year after year, their disturbing influence is minimized because it can be foreseen.

In the United States the situation is very different. Fluctuations in government money holdings over short periods are perhaps not more considerable than in European countries, but the average amount of such holdings has for many years been enormously greater, with the possible exception of Russia, and of Japan during and just after the recent war. Changes in our revenue laws are made at infrequent intervals, and appropriations are authorized with little reference to probable income. Fluctuations in the amount of government funds are therefore of a wholly different character from those in European countries. In 1905 the Treasury cash holdings,[1] exclusive of trust funds, and the $150,000,000 gold reserve, were nearly stationary. During 1906 and the greater part of 1907 there was a steady upward movement, which carried the amount of government money from $240,-000,000 to more than $390,000,000. Since that time the tendency has been quite as strong in the opposite direction, and in September, 1910, the Treasury held only $160,000,000. Throughout nearly all this period the Treasury held more than the maximum balances of England, France, and Germany taken together and for much of this time more than the total deposits of all kinds of the Bank of England

In magnitude, permanence, and in the nature of their fluctuations, the balances of the United States government are clearly quite unlike those of other countries. Placed in a central bank, they would constitute a permanent fund of widely varying proportions, the use of which would give the bank a fluctuating power unlike anything in banking experience. But the manner of putting these funds into general use would be equally without precedent. Without doubt there would be a general demand that the deposits be used with some degree of approxima-

[1] The figures in the text are in each instance rather more than a hundred million dollars greater than the monthly returns of available cash in the Treasury, which offsets against cash holdings such current obligations as disbursing officers' balances.

tion to the population and the supposed needs of different parts of the country. At this point an insurmountable obstacle would be encountered. To lend directly to the business community, even if that were to be permitted, would require an impossible number of branches. Lending at the relatively small number of branches which we have assumed might be established would not accomplish the purpose. Here the example of the Bank of England fails to supply a precedent because of what may be termed the lack of fluidity in our system of credit. In England, and indeed in all countries which have central banks, it matters little whether the central bank makes loans in a single place or generally throughout the country. If, for example, the Bank of England makes advances in London, it relieves the pressure for loans upon the other banks. They are then in position to lend more freely at any of their numerous branches where there may be an active demand. The entire country is served by the several thousand branches of less than one hundred banks, most of which have their head office in London. Similar concentration, and in some instances to an even greater extent, is found in other European countries. In the United States banks are not permitted to operate branches under the national and most state banking laws. Consequent absence of banking concentration rather than the absence of a central bank is the most fundamental difference between banking in this and other countries. Elsewhere the central bank is simply the final step in banking systems, which without it would in any case be highly centralized.[1] How fundamentally important is this preliminary concentration in securing effective results from central banks of the European type will appear in our analysis of each of their various activities.

In order to distribute its funds widely, the central bank would be obliged to lend to at least as many banks as there are localities; and, since the selection of a single bank would give rise to charges of favoritism, the bank would be certain to lend to all the banks. There are now over seven thousand banks in the national system, and, if any distinct advantage were to follow, the State banks would doubtless generally enter the system. The central bank would be obliged to decide between the claims of twenty thousand or more banks. To estimate the quality of the securities offered by the various banks would be no easy problem, tho slight compared with the difficulty of determining the amount to be lent to each bank. How determine the relative needs of a large New York or Chicago bank on the one hand, and of rural banks in Wisconsin or Texas on the other? Loan contraction, when thought desirable upon general grounds, would be a yet more delicate undertaking. The withdrawal of credit from a single reservoir reduces the general level. If a given quantity is to be taken from thousands of reservoirs, it becomes necessary to consider the supply in each, and to fix upon those which can endure the loss without dan-

[1] There, is, indeed, comparatively little banking concentration in Japan. But the Bank of Japan has unusual powers of control, owing to the scarcity of capital in that country. The other banks are ordinarily obliged to resort to it for loans. Moreover, public opinion has not forced the Bank to make advances to the banks generally. See the article on Japanese banking by the writer in the publications of the National Monetary Commission.

gerous shrinkage. Consideration must also be given
to the likelihood that complaints will be made that
neighboring reservoirs have not contributed their
fair quota. From whatever side the subject is ap-
proached there seems no escape from the conclusion
that a central bank would not be able to handle the
deposits of the government if their amount was large
in such a manner as to give general satisfaction and
escape general criticism. It is not improbable that
they would have to be distributed in some more or
less permanent fashion analogous to our existing
arrangement tho of course the process would be different, through loans, not by direct deposits.

The root of the difficulty, it will be observed, is
found in the handling of the loan account of the Bank
when the power to extend credit is due to causes
which would give color of reasonableness to demands
for its general application throughout the country at
rates which would be profitable for borrowing banks.
This difficulty would not, however, prove serious if
the deposits of the government can be kept from
exceeding a fair working balance. This can be readily
accomplished, if the present relationship between
the bank note and government bonds is severed. It
would then be a simple matter to use such surplus as
might accrue in the redemption or purchase of the
bonds.[1]

An elastic currency is the panacea which has been
most generally prescribed for our financial ills, and it
is largely because a central bank is believed to be an

[1] For a simple method of bringing this separation about, see pp. 128-132.

effective means to this end that its adoption has been urged. This is not, indeed, always a function of central banks. The Bank of England cannot increase its note issues except by impounding an exactly equivalent amount of gold in its issue department. Elsewhere the monopoly of issue is subject to less drastic restriction, and the notes are a true credit currency, expanding and contracting with variations in business requirements. Confining our attention to the use of notes in normal periods and taking for consideration France, in which the check habit is not very general, it appears that the average volume of notes in circulation has steadily increased and is now nearly five thousand million francs, and the difference between the maximum and the minimum amount in circulation in a year is often as much as five hundred million francs. In England, where deposit banking is familiar to all, there are no such wide variations in the demand for currency, the amount of money of all kinds in circulation fluctuating within the extremely narrow limits of three million pounds. In the United States the use of checks is quite as general as in Great Britain, but the relatively greater importance of agriculture causes wider seasonal variations in the demand for money. The steady growth of the check habit in purely rural communities seems, however, to be causing a relative decline in this demand. Notwithstanding increased agricultural production and higher prices, it shows no tendency to increase, tho it varies much from year to year. The national bank returns for the last ten years indicate an autumnal requirement at most of about $50,000,000. A somewhat greater shifting of funds between banks doubtless occurs, as the banks in the crop-growing regions naturally increase their money holdings rather more than the actual outflow. In any event, our seasonal requirements are certainly well within the limits of the circulation of the Bank of France, and there is fair ground for maintaining that they could be supplied by an institution with similar powers, if there were no other obstacles beyond mere magnitude to be taken into the account.

Our difficulties would appear, as in the case of government deposits, as soon as the attempt was made to place the notes only where in normal times they are really needed, — in agricultural sections of the country. It would be a comparatively simple matter to send notes to the crop-growing regions, just as money is now shipped by the banks of the money centers. But if a central bank were to issue notes, the demand for them in periods of active trade would not be confined to the crop-moving period or to banks in agricultural regions. When a single bank has the monopoly of issue the notes acquire somewhat more the full characteristics of money than is the case when notes are issued by many competing banks. In particular they are almost equally serviceable for purposes of reserve against deposit liabilities. It is reasonable to expect, therefore, that bankers generally would be eager to secure them. As in the case of government deposits, the central bank would be forced to decide between the conflicting claims of thousands of banks, each urging its own local needs. Once more the absence of branch banking presents itself as a formidable, it would seem even insuperable, obstacle to the successful exercise of an important function of all central banks of the European type except the Bank of England.

It cannot be too strongly insisted upon that the experience of other countries with notes issued freely by a central bank affords no adequate indication of the probable effects of such an issue in the United States. There is a wide difference between Anglo-Saxon countries and the countries of Continental Europe in the extent to which checks are used, and consequently in the possibility of credit expansion in the form of deposits. Changes in the deposits of French or German banks, for example, are almost entirely due to the direct receipt or payment of cash or notes. In England and in the United States the principal cause of change in the deposits of commercial banks, especially during periods of active business, is the increase or decrease in the volume of loans. The borrower ordinarily wants a credit at the bank against which he can issue checks, and those who receive the checks have equally little occasion for actual cash. The significance of this difference can best be shown by an illustration. When deposits increase in German banks, we may be reasonably certain that they have more money to lend, and that, when they make loans, they are obliged to pay out more money or notes. When American banks have more deposits, it usually means that they have already increased their loans. In Germany, if a bank secures through rediscounts notes from the Reichsbank and makes further loans on its own account, it will find

that, aside from stock exchange and other dealings
of a similar description, it can lend but little more
than the amount of the notes. In the United States
the notes of a central bank would serve as a basis
for deposit credit to several times their amount.[1]

Aside from periods of general trade depression, it
is highly improbable that the notes of a central bank
would speedily return to it when once put out in
circulation, except when the central bank contracted
its loans. The process of contraction would be disturbing, because it would involve a contraction several
times as great in the loans of other banks. The conclusion would seem to be inevitable that with a highly
developed deposit credit system the note of a central
bank, if issued in any considerable volume, is a dangerous instrument, tending towards inflation. It
has apparently been some more or less well-thought-
out reasoning of this nature that has led the best
English opinion to oppose proposals that the Bank
of England be allowed to issue a credit bank note.

As in the case of government deposits, these difficulties would be greatly diminished, if a central bank
can be devised which will strengthen our banking
system in some other way than through the possession
and exercise of an enormous lending power. This
power, especially if derived from a monopoly of issue
under conditions which would permit the Bank to put
out a large volume of notes, could not fail to bring
upon it an irresistible demand for accommodation from
all quarters in periods of active business. The possi-

---

[1] Balances with the Bank would also have a similar effect in so far as they might
come to be regarded as reserves by the other banks.

bilities of a central bank of limited scope will be considered in the final chapter. At this stage the question may, however, be raised whether it is entirely desirable that there should be a system of issue which shall free the banks entirely from occasional moderate requirements for actual cash. The deposit is an obligation for payment on demand, and the actual demand for cash serves to remind bankers of that very important fact. It enforces a sort of taking account of stock, and brings home to bankers the necessity of keeping their house in order at all times. Where deposit banking is not general, doubtless credit in the form of bank notes should be not only elastic but also capable of permanent expansion. But for countries like England and the United States restrictions on note issue exercise a much-needed restraining influence, through the increased demand for money for every-day use which always accompanies business activity and rising prices.[1]

II

THE PRECAUTIONARY STAGE

The husbanding of resources which has been emphasized as an essential feature of the policy of central banks in normal times might be thought to belong to the second or precautionary stage of their operations. For purposes of exposition, however, there is some advantage to be gained by simply grouping in this stage actual steps taken by central banks

[1] This matter was discussed by the writer in the Quarterly Journal of Economics for August, 1904, pp. 513-528.

to restrain the expansion of credit and to strengthen
their reserves. The essence of the distinction is that
in the first stage the central bank, however carefully
it may husband its own resources, leaves the market
free to follow its own course, while in the second
stage it endeavors to subject the market to a certain
measure of control.

In the exercise of this function a central bank seeks
to govern the market by the wise combination of
persuasion and control. A variety of devices are
resorted to, in part dependent upon the circumstances
of the particular case and in part the result of customs
and traditions which have been developed in different
countries. Some of these devices are entirely within
the direct sphere of operation of the central bank,
while others require the co-operation of the other
banks or the control of their operations. The Bank
of France has relied in the past largely upon the device,
peculiar to itself, of a premium upon gold withdrawn
for export. In Germany the Reichsbank is said to
have prevented gold exports by agreement with other
banks, even when there would be a clear and immediate profit from the operation. Many of the central
banks facilitate gold imports by advances upon gold
in transit. The Bank of England can within narrow
limits change its buying and selling prices for gold
in bars and for foreign coin. Most of the Continental
central banks regularly hold considerable quantities
of foreign bills, which can be used to check gold exports and to secure gold imports. This device is the
main reliance of the Bank of Belgium; it is of very
great importance in the case of the Bank of Austria-

Hungary; and it seems to be regarded with increasing favor at the Reichsbank. Its effectiveness would largely disappear if it were universally adopted. It is noteworthy that the bulk of the foreign bills thus held are upon London, to which the rest of the world seems to look more and more as the one certain and immediate resource in times of emergency.

One device, however, the sliding scale of discount, is made use of by all central banks, and, with hardly an exception, is of pre-eminent importance.

The primary object of an advance in the rate of discount is to influence foreign exchange rates, to check gold exports or to stimulate gold imports, by increasing the investment holdings by foreign banks of bills drawn upon the country. A quite secondary object is to diminish the demand for domestic loans. Success is always dependent upon whether the market rate follows the bank rate. To bring this about is the most frequent, if not the most serious, task of a central bank. When the strain upon the reserve is merely anticipated or of moderate proportions, it is frequently difficult to make the market follow the bank. If the other banks have abundant funds and if the necessity of caution is not obvious, the immediate effect of the advance of the bank rate upon the market rate may be imperceptible. The central bank will then secure little new business. In countries where its proportion of the lending business is large, it is true that the increased demand for loans at the other banks will soon force up the market rate. But, as has already been pointed out, the business of central banks has become small in proportion to the total credit business in most countries. It has happened with increasing frequency that the outside market has been able to shoulder the entire lending business without advancing rates to the point desired by the central banks. In recent years both the Bank of England and the Bank of Germany have found it necessary with increasing frequency to deprive the market of its surplus funds. This is accomplished in England by the sale of government securities, and in Germany by the rediscounting of Treasury bills. This device has answered its purpose to a striking degree. Its effectiveness is a direct consequence of the narrow foundation of balances with the central bank, upon which rest the vast liabilities of the other banks. In London, for example, it is supposed that bankers' balances may amount to half the total deposits of the Bank of England, say £25,000,000. If these balances are reduced even by a million pounds through the sale of government securities by the Bank of England,[1] the other banks are obliged to contract their loans and reduce their deposits by many times that amount, in order to preserve the customary proportion of balances to their credit liabilities. The credit structure is so delicately poised upon its foundation of Bank of England balances that it is sensitive to very slight influences.

While the responsibilities of central banks are increasing, the most important instrument at their

[1] The balances of the other banks would almost certainly be reduced by this step unless the securities were sold to individual depositors of the Bank of England. If the securities were purchased by the other banks or by their customers, checks in payment would swell the clearing-house exchanges of the Bank of England. If they were sold to bill brokers or their customers, the result would be the same, tho there would be one or more additional transfers of credit required to complete the operation.

disposal in the performance of their heavy duties has not become more effective. No specific instance has yet occurred to show that the burden has become too great, probably because the principles which should govern a central bank have become more clearly understood by bankers and the public, and a tradition has been developed which makes it possible for the central bank in most instances to govern by persuasion rather than resort to force.

Many English observers have questioned whether the extent to which the concentration of reserves has been carried does not seriously imperil the foundation of the entire financial structure. The heavy burden upon the reserve of the Bank of England makes the London money market exceedingly sensitive to even slight temporary influences, especially those which may cause the withdrawal of gold for export. The discount rate is advanced more frequently than would probably be necessary if reserves were larger. Repeated efforts have been made to secure united action among the London joint stock banks, looking towards the provision of some reserve in their vaults or a special reserve deposit at the Bank of England. Altho this change might strengthen the system in some respects, it is also probable that the market would then less easily be brought to follow the lead of the central bank in its discount policy.

Since every unusual demand for money falls upon the central bank, it would be to its advantage, were that possible, to eliminate the dishonest and reckless management of particular banks. History does not afford any clear indication that central banks have been able to effect much in this direction. It might also be expected that something would be accomplished by example and precept to moderate general tendencies towards the dangerously rapid expansion of credit by the banks as a whole, but here also it would be difficult to cite specific instances of successful endeavor.[1] General speculative movements are less violent in Europe than in the United States, but this difference is properly ascribable to the greater opportunities for rapid development in a new country with large undeveloped natural resources. Germany, which in late years has been in manufactures and commerce virtually a new country, has experienced highly speculative movements, which the Reichsbank has been seemingly powerless to control. After all, a central bank can do little more than husband its own resources for the future, at a time when the other banks have abundant funds and a spirit of general over-confidence pervades the business community.

All the devices made use of by central banks, as they exist in other countries, in the precautionary stage of their policy have one common characteristic; they are designed mainly to improve matters by influencing the foreign exchanges. The prevention of a foreign drain and the attraction of gold from other countries is the principal object in view. Little direct influence can be brought to bear to strengthen the domestic banking situation by reducing the aggregate of credit advances. In times of great business

---

[1] In the autumn of 1906 the Bank of England was able to secure a discontinuance of the enormous advances being made by London bankers to New York financiers by means of finance bills.

or speculative activity, very high discount rates may
reduce somewhat the demand for loans for purely
domestic purposes, but not necessarily, or even probably, the demand for those which are most undesirable.
Foreign borrowing alone is likely to be diminished
to an appreciable extent by the ordinary advances
in rates. The negotiation of finance bills by foreign
bankers may be made unprofitable, and the holding
of commercial bills for investment abroad may be
increased. By this means the total volume of loans
in a market constituted like that of London may be
considerably diminished. The foreign trade and financial operations of the leading European countries are
of enormous magnitude, both absolutely and relative
to the total business of those countries. Many of
the great crises during the nineteenth century were
precipitated, and at least in part caused, by events
occurring in other parts of the world with which
Europe has close financial relations. The purely
domestic economic activities of old countries are
comparatively stable, and seldom give occasion to
inordinate speculation. Any arrangement, therefore,
which succeeds both in strengthening the central
bank and also in placing a somewhat restraining
influence upon foreign speculative operations, is one
which affords protection against the most serious
weakness threatening the European financial world.

When we turn to the United States, we find a situation strikingly and fundamentally different from that
which we have just described. Our financial troubles
are of domestic origin. Not one of our crises has
been precipitated by events occurring in other coun-

tries.[1] Our foreign trade and investments, compared
with those of European countries, form a small part of
our total economic activities. Our exports of food-
stuffs and raw materials have a broad and fairly
stable market, while our imports, largely of luxuries,
respond quickly to every change in the consuming
power of the people. We have no appreciable amount
of capital invested abroad, and a diminishing proportion of capital employed in the country is of foreign
origin. Moreover, we do not finance any considerable share of our foreign trade. Bills drawn against
our exports are usually discounted in Europe, and
our imports are secured through commercial letters
of credit, which also give rise to bills which are accepted and discounted in European money centers. The
element of weakness in our foreign exchange position
is found in the enormous temporary obligations incurred during periods of active business by American
bankers through the issue of finance bills. If a central bank is to strengthen our credit structure, it is
certainly not to be accomplished by the attraction
of further amounts of foreign money through high
discount rates, at least not until we shall have begun
to finance a considerable portion of our foreign trade.

In only one way does it seem possible that a central bank might secure assistance from foreign sources
without an addition to our current obligations. It
might conceivably in normal times hold a large amount
of foreign commercial bills instead of following the
present custom of sending them abroad at once for

[1] The Baring failure in 1890 greatly increased the usual strain of the autumn
months in New York; but, tho economic conditions were far from satisfactory in
the United States, no crisis occurred.

discount. This policy would, however, be regarded as a menace in European markets to be guarded against at all cost. It would not in the slightest degree enable the central bank to exert a restraining influence on domestic business activities. It would be simply a device to draw more money from Europe in emergencies, — a power which is already the most disturbing factor in the European money market.[1]

Our financial troubles are almost wholly due to causes which may be traced to our domestic economic activities. In periods of prosperity the expansion of loans is peculiarly rapid, because of the abundant opportunities for development in a new country. It would be incumbent upon a central bank to control or moderate this tendency, especially when borrowers were using the proceeds of loans in hazardous speculative enterprises or were relying upon them to supply deficiencies in working capital. Raising the rate of discount after the European practice would not avail. It does not have any considerable effect in this direction even in Europe, except upon loans of foreign origin.

Even such a slight moderating influence as an advance in the rate of discount may have elsewhere upon the volume of purely domestic loans would probably be lacking in this country, because there is every reason to fear that the central bank could not make its rate effective throughout the country. In preceding pages we have seen that a variety of

[1] This subject is again referred to in the final chapter, see p. 169. It is to be hoped that an American central bank would stand on its own bottom like the Bank of England and that it would hold foreign bills only in order to employ idle funds, not as an emergency resource.

influences are present in countries with central banks, which give them some control over market rates. Among these may be mentioned prevalent banking customs, a delicately poised money market, fluidity of credit, the possession by the central bank in normal times of some share in the current loans to individuals, and a condition of constant dependence upon it in the case of the other banks. No one of these factors taken alone is indispensable, but in the absence of any one of them the others must be correspondingly more powerful.

Banking customs, such as the relation of the interest rate on deposits to the bank rate, cannot be created off-hand. They were the product of slow growth at a time when central banks occupied a commanding position and when other banks were in the course of development. Loans to individual borrowers are to be expressly forbidden, at least those which would involve competition with other banks. The fluidity of credit is absent in this country, and will remain absent while we wisely continue to prefer banks managed by persons with extensive local knowledge to branch banks subject to bureaucratic managers, acting under general rules laid down at a distant head office. For this reason we cannot expect our numerous money markets to be subject to a single sliding scale of discount. It would be necessary for the Bank to lend at widely different rates in the different sections of the country; otherwise an excessive portion of its resources would be absorbed in the West and South.

The advocates of the central bank proposal have
been impressed with the defects in our banking system
in times of emergency and have sought earnestly
for a remedy, but, unfortunately, they have overlooked the effects of a bank of this kind in normal
times and especially when precautionary measures
may serve to minimize an emergency and even prevent
its occurrence. A bank with large lending power,
lending only to other banks, would have one fundamental defect, so serious as to destroy its power of
usefulness. It would not be able to exert a restraining
influence upon the expansion of credit, because it
would have no means of carrying out a precautionary
policy. Bearing in mind what has been said on previous pages,[1] the consequences of an issue of notes
by a bank of this kind will be readily understood.
Is it not certain that, in the eager search for funds
in times of active business, the other banks would
resort to it for heavy loans? Doubtless a considerable
measure of accommodation would have been thus
granted if we had possessed such a central bank in
the years before the crisis of 1907, even tho it had
been managed with far more conservatism than we
have any reason to be certain of securing at all times.[2]
Every dollar thus borrowed would have been an
addition to the extension of credit at a time when
restraint was needed, not expansion. The central
bank would have been creating a certain amount
of credit expansion, which its later power of con-

[1] See pp. 36-38.
[2] Recent history affords no assurance that the government influence in the management of a central bank would be always found on the conservative side. See the
article on "The Banks and the Treasury under Secretary Shaw," by Professor A. P.
Andrew, in the Quarterly Journal of Economics for August, 1907.

traction could certainly not have exceeded and probably could not have equalled, because the volume of credit cannot suddenly be largely diminished without serious disturbance. The power to issue notes by a bank of this kind would be a positive evil unless it were almost entirely reserved for use only upon occasions of actual emergency.

The possession of the bankers' deposits might, at first sight, be expected to give the proposed central bank some control over the expansion of credit. If it should secure the bulk of the bankers' deposits now held in reserve and central reserve cities, it would then keep unquestionably a larger reserve against these deposits than is held by existing banks. With these deposits and the government balances a central bank might be able at the outset to acquire a commanding position in the banking world. The other banks generally might be forced to resort to it for accommodation, and, since the loans of the reserve and central reserve city banks would have been greatly diminished on account of the loss of bankers' deposits, no net expansion of credit might follow. It is by no means certain or even probable, however, that the other banks would remain permanently dependent upon the central bank after a sufficient time had elapsed for new capital to enter the banking field. From that moment its power of restraint would cease.

It is unnecessary to discuss further the possibilities of a bank conceived upon these lines. Aside from the extremely doubtful results which might follow from its activities, it is unthinkable that any one, much less those concerned with the management

of our existing banks, would be prepared to see our
entire credit system become constantly and directly
dependent upon a single institution. It has been
given passing notice, because it illustrates very clearly
the practical impossibility of securing through the
manipulation of the loan account of a central bank
anything like effective guidance or control of the
credit operations of a system composed of many
thousands of banks.

One proposal,[1] which has received a very favorable
public reception, does not involve the loss of any
bankers' deposits by existing banks; but provides
for the creation of more deposits of this kind. The
central bank is to hold a part of the reserves now
held in the form of cash by the banks of the three
central reserve cities. Upon the basis of the funds
thus secured, together with those provided through
its large capital and government deposits and by
means of the issue of notes, the bank would be able
to engage in business of imposing dimensions, but
its power to restrain would be subject to all the ob-
stacles which have been mentioned above. At the
outset its establishment would not involve any diminution whatever in the credits granted by the other
banks. Restricted to dealings with them its loans
would at once enable the other banks to lend more
freely. Let us suppose that such a bank had been
established soon after the recent panic, would it have
found a desirable outlet for its funds at a time when
rates for commercial paper were often at four per

---

[1] See the presidential address of Geo. M. Reynolds before the 1909 convention of
the American Bankers' Association.

cent. or less and when call-loan rates were frequently below one per cent. ?   In no way could it have controlled the employment for speculative purposes of the vast amount of funds which accumulated in the New York banks.   At the present time, when business activities are increasing, it would indeed find many banking applicants for loans but can it be argued that the country requires more rapid expansion of credit than can be provided by existing institutions ? Surely all our experience goes to show that credit has always been extended with dangerous rapidity during periods when hope and confidence possessed the business world.   If this country were but scantily supplied with banking facilities the proposal would have far more to recommend it.   For then the other banks would be constantly under the control of the central institution.   In the actual situation of affairs in this country the central bank, to be a vital restraining force, must take away an appreciable portion of their business from existing banks, so that its advances to them will not be a basis for undesirable credit expansion.

There remains a further alternative for consideration. Altho a central bank might be unable to exert a restraining influence upon the expansion of credit, through its lending operations it may be urged that by refraining from the issue of its notes in ordinary times and by maintaining a large reserve it would increase the power of the banks to cope with emergencies.   A familiar illustration will make evident the undesirable consequences which would follow the establishment of a central bank of such restricted

scope unless coupled with provisions designed to
strengthen existing banks and to secure the use of
their resources in emergencies. For many years
we have had something of the kind in the independent
Treasury system. During much of its history it
has held surplus funds which have been turned over
to the banks in times of real or fancied need. The
banks have not been obliged to depend entirely upon
their own resources, and have not, therefore, given
sufficient heed to indications of approaching emergency.
Let us not delude ourselves with the notion that a
central bank of this kind, which would be a mere
crutch, would be able to achieve results similar to
those which have been secured in countries where
the central bank is the very heart of the credit organism.
Some share in the loans made directly to the business
community or a condition of constant dependence
for the other banks (as in Japan) is absolutely essential,
if a central bank is to be able to exert a restraining
influence through its loan account. Otherwise it
will simply play the rôle of the unwise parent whose
indulgence weakens the sense of responsibility and
lightens the penalty for lack of foresight.[1]

[1] The example of the Second Bank of the United States has been thought by
many to show that a central bank would be feasible in this country at the present time.
But conditions are so radically different that the results achieved by it do not establish
a precedent. The Second Bank, except in its first years, succeeded in a measure
in restraining the credit operations of other banks. Its business was of far greater
magnitude than that of any other bank, and also considerable in proportion to the
total of banking business. It was able to restrain the other banks because in the
normal course of business it was a creditor but not a lender in relation to them. By
contracting its own loans it was able to bring pressure to bear upon them by sending
in their notes for redemption. Few of the other banks seem to have carried any
considerable reserve either in cash or in the form of balances with the central institution.
In times of stress they regularly resorted to it for accommodation. The chief business
of the Second Bank was, however, with the business community and not with the
banks. Moreover, its note issue did not serve as a basis for an indefinitely large

The many difficulties which would confront a central bank seeking to strengthen our banking system through the use of an enormous lending power would seem to be insurmountable. These difficulties would, however, disappear if government deposits are kept down to a moderate working balance, if the right to issue notes is carefully restricted, and if the other banks continue to hold their own reserves. Assuming also that as a preliminary measure legislation is adopted designed to strengthen existing banks, the ground would then be ready for the construction of a central bank of limited scope and moderate lending power provided such an institution seems likely to be of material advantage. This is a question which can be answered to more purpose after an examination of the activities of existing central banks during crises.

III

THE ACTIVITIES OF CENTRAL BANKS DURING CRISES

Analysis of the activities of European central banks during periods of acute financial strain cannot be separated from the consideration of their normal and steady operations. If in normal times and during periods of moderate strain such an institution does not seem likely to fit into our system, it becomes

credit structure in the form of deposits, because this form of banking was not at that time largely developed. Finally, it may be mentioned that the life of the Second Bank was cut short before the crisis of 1837, so that we have no means of determining what it was capable of doing in a disturbance of first-class proportions. For a sympathetic and detailed account of the service of the bank in strengthening the credit system, see R. C. H. Catterall, The Second Bank of the United States, chapter XIX.

obviously out of the question to seek by this means a remedy for more acute financial disturbances. But the success which has crowned the efforts of central banks in handling crises suggests the wisdom of studying their methods, with the object of applying them to our own situation, if perchance they may prove to be independent of any particular form of banking organization.

In times of severe financial strain the central bank plays an active dominating rôle. Upon it rests the responsibility for maintaining specie payments, and also in large measure for the continuance of lending facilities to the business community. This responsibility was not clearly recognized, and the policy which should be followed in such situations was not clearly understood in the latter part of the eighteenth century and the early years of the nineteenth century. In some instances, loans were restricted, with disastrous consequences not only to business, but to the central banks as well. In other instances, loans were granted freely, but without that concomitant advance in the rate of discount required to influence foreign exchange rates and to drive away borrowers whose needs were not urgent.[1] For the last forty years at least the policy which should be followed has been clearly understood, largely owing to Bagehot's reiterated expositions in the *Economist*, finally embodied in more permanent form in his *Lombard Street*.

The policy of liberal loans, tho at high rates, and the payment of money or notes to all depositors who

[1] MacLeod's Theory and Practice of Banking contains the best account of English banking experience during crises before 1860. See chapters ix, xi, and xii.

for any reason whatever may require cash, are now everywhere recognized as the guiding principles of action in emergencies. More recently still another method of relief has been adopted in practice, if not in theory. Central banks have at times taken the lead, as in the Baring instance, in arrangements for the conservation of the assets of large banks which are not hopelessly insolvent, and by preventing sudden liquidation have confined the disturbance within narrow limits. The machinery for united action will hardly be set in motion in the absence of some person or institution of commanding influence in whom the business community has confidence. In this matter the central bank is somewhat superior to the clearing-house organization in American cities. In carrying out the crisis policy as to loans and cash, a central bank does not require any previous agreement with the other banks. Whether the same course of action can be followed in the United States, where in the absence of a central bank such agreement is necessary, and, if so, with equally good results, is the problem which now presents itself for examination.

In one important respect the course of American crises has been strikingly unlike many of those in Europe. The foreign exchange situation has not been the storm center in the United States. Even in 1893, when our currency was redundant through causes beyond the control of the banks, the export of gold was an influence in precipitating the crisis, primarily because the intention as well as the ability of the government to maintain the gold standard was doubtful. Moreover, we have never experienced any difficulty in securing abundant supplies of gold from Europe after the outbreak of crises. As early as 1857 we were able to import over $6,000,-000 in the course of a few weeks, — an amount which was equal to about half the reserves of the New York banks at that time. The enormous importation of about $100,000,000 in 1907 is within the recollection of all. It has been argued that the heavy importations of 1907, as well as those during some of the other crises, are in part to be attributed to the currency premium, which made it possible to import gold at a profit, even when exchange rates were above the normal export point. But it is important to observe that gold exports were engaged before there was any premium upon currency. Moreover, only so far as foreign exchange rates which were quoted in the medium of certified checks failed to advance *pari passu* with the depreciation of the checks, was the currency premium a factor in the situation. After all, the movement of commodities and foreign credits are the principal influences determining gold movements, and neither of them is strengthened by the suspension of cash payments by the banks and the consequent currency premium.[1] Forced sales of commodities and securities have indeed provided much of the necessary exchange, but on the other hand gold imports have been upon an extraordinary scale.

[1] The gold imported during the crisis of 1907 was almost entirely secured through the discount of trade bills. During the spring and summer months it had been impossible to negotiate the usual amount of anticipatory bills in Europe. Consequently, the enormous autumn sales of American commodities abroad provided the means of payment for the gold which was imported.

Certainly the foreign exchange situation would not prove troublesome in a crisis so handled as not to subject industry and trade to intolerably severe pressure.

Much importance has been ascribed by those who favor a central bank to the absence of the domestic bill of exchange and of the bank acceptance in the American business world. It is urged that satisfactory results through the operations of a central bank cannot be secured unless the bill of exchange comes into general use, and that its absence is a fundamental cause of the lack of liquidness in the assets of the banks.[1] But, in drawing this conclusion, form rather than substance has been regarded. Bills of exchange are more liquid than other assets in emergencies, because the central banks are more willing to take that form of security. The main essential is that a central bank shall not have exhausted its power to lend before the emergency occurs. The experience of the clearing houses in connection with the issue of loan certificates shows that our banks have abundant security to offer, if there were some reservoir of unused credit at which it could be exchanged for some kind of acceptable purchasing power.

With regard to the continuance of loans during crises the defects in the working of our banking system

[1] The bill of exchange has a certain vogue, because it arises out of business transactions, the termination of which will in due course provide the means of payment. This is by no means always the case, however. The accommodation bill was more than a bugbear to bankers of former generations, and in recent years the bill, accepted by one bank and discounted at another bank, has provided the means for highly speculative undertakings. The extensive use of such bills in Germany before 1907 weakened the entire credit structure, altho through a happy combination of good fortune and skilful management the threatened collapse was avoided. See W. Prion, Das deutsche Wechselgeschäft, pp. 150, 189, 242, and Deutsche Oekonomist, 1908, pp. 456, 489.

appear at first sight extremely serious. Not only during crises, but also in years of less serious strain, rates for loans have soared to extraordinary levels far beyond anything known in other countries; and at times reports are current that no loans can be secured upon any terms. More careful examination of the facts will show that this impression is not a little exaggerated. The banks in general have always taken care of their regular customers, often exacting no advance on the rates at which they have been accustomed to lend. The best borrowers will not pay the high rates prevailing in the general loan market and demand of their own banks accommodation at moderate rates. The borrowers who have experienced great difficulty are those who depend entirely upon the distribution of their paper to many banks through note brokers, and those who borrow upon call or time against collateral securities for investment or speculative purposes. The statistics of the loans of the national banks which appear in the reports of the Comptroller of the Currency afford conclusive evidence that no wholesale and rapid curtailment of loans has taken place even in months of extreme panic. Between May and October in 1893 the total loans of the national banks were reduced from $2,161,-000,000 to $1,843,000,000, slightly more than 15 per cent. But during that period, chiefly because of failures, the number of banks was reduced from 3,830 to 3,781, thus accounting for at least a part of the loan reduction. Moreover, this contraction was apparently spread pretty evenly over the entire period of five months. The July returns show that loans had been reduced by $140,000,000, leaving $180,000,000 to be accounted for in the three succeeding months. In 1907 there were comparatively few bank failures, and the general economic situation was far less unsatisfactory. Between August and December, 1907, loans were reduced from $4,678,000,000 to $4,585,-000,000, almost exactly 2 per cent. In many of the cities of the country there was a slight increase in loans. In New York the loans of the national banks increased from $712,000,000 to $775,000,000, altho, on account of the difficulties of the trust companies, it is probable that there was no actual increase of loans in that city.

The contraction of loans would therefore seem to be wholly incommensurate with the commotion in the loan market which characterizes our crises. Sudden liquidation would be prevented by very moderate advances by a central bank. The banks do indeed make an effort to convert their loans into money, but this effort is not successful. Each bank follows the course which is effective when a smaller number of banks find it necessary to diminish their liabilities. Let us take the call loan as an example. When a few banks demand the payment of these loans, the brokers, to whom they are principally made, secure loans elsewhere, and the banks calling the loans are paid. The total volume of call loans is not much changed. Within narrow limits it may be possible to reduce the aggregate of such loans by sales of securities to persons able to pay for them outright. It is also possible to secure additional margins from customers for whom brokers are carrying securities. But when all banks call their loans, they cease to be convertible into money. Purchasers who might be able to pay for securities outright become frightened, and little or no contraction takes place, while panic and alarm are generally increased. It usually becomes necessary to form a money pool, as was the case in the first week of the panic of 1907. This is nothing more than an agreement among banks to bring about what the banks in ordinary times do without agreement. In European countries the call loan, as well as other loans, is convertible, not because it is paid, but because the central banks stand ready to supply the necessary credit to borrowers whose obligations must be met. In this country it should be more clearly understood that here also no class of loans, not even call loans, can be diminished suddenly to any considerable amount. A given volume of business cannot suddenly be deprived of that amount of credit with which it has been customarily carried on. Attempts to do so involve direct loss, not only to borrowers, but to the banks, and they also weaken public confidence, which more than the cash reserve is the real foundation of any system of credit.[1]

The clearing house loan certificate is a device similar in its purpose to the money pool. The latter secures the continuance of loans from day to day for a particular purpose. The clearing house loan certificate

[1] Another cause of violent fluctuations in the rates for call loans is quite independent of our banking methods. In all European stock exchanges, dealings are with reference to fixed settlement dates, either fortnightly or monthly. Our method of daily stock delivery involves constant shifting of loans, which is a serious menace in times of crisis. It explains more than all other causes the fluctuations in call loan rates in this country. It also causes sudden and unnecessary fluctuations in the quoted prices of shares, and stimulates the attempts of speculators to corner particular stocks.

is designed to insure the continuance of loans of all kinds throughout the period of an emergency. It was devised after the crisis of 1857, which brought home to the New York banks the disastrous consequences of the policy of loan contraction to themselves, as well as to the business community. The banks had been unable to agree upon a liberal loan policy, because of the fear of unfavorable clearing house balances, which would have to be met by banks making loans freely to banks which pursued a more selfish policy. The clearing house loan certificate makes it possible for banks to lend freely, without fearing the loss of cash on this account. It takes away much of the advantage which might be derived by banks which restricted their loans. The issue of these certificates does not in the slightest diminish the obligation to pay individual depositors their money on demand, or the obligation to pay banking depositors outside the clearing house association. It is a device which in its origin had reference primarily and solely to the lending policy, not to the reserve policy of the banks. The clearing house loan certificate is absolutely essential, in the absence of a central bank, to secure united action as regards loans during a crisis, and it has never failed to be fairly adequate for the purpose. Unfortunately, the use of this device alone seems to involve, or at least to hasten, the suspension of cash payments by the banks, and, on this account, it must be confessed that the remedy is quite as bad or even worse than the disease which it is designed to cure.[1]

[1] The relation between the use of loan certificates and suspensions is considered later, see pp. 106–113.

The issue of loan certificates does not diminish the amount of money held by the banks of a city taken as a whole. But if the certificates are taken out and used by all the banks in the payment of clearing house balances, banks having large favorable balances may be forced to suspend through the withdrawal of cash especially by country banks, which have built up their deposits in one bank mainly with checks and drafts drawn on the other banks.

Suspension, when limited to payments to individual depositors whose requirements are largely local, is comparatively harmless. But our city banks have another class of depositors to whom their obligations are, at least in New York, nearly as great as those to their individual depositors. Reference is, of course, made to deposits of outside banks. Most of the requirements of the individual depositor can be served with checks payable through the clearing house. But when a distant bank demands the return of the reserve which it has on deposit with the city bank, nothing short of actual cash will serve the purpose. Failure to meet such demands fully and without delay precipitates suspension everywhere. Moreover, it has an incomparably greater disturbing effect upon business activities. Purely local business, aside from pay-rolls, can be carried on after a fashion with checks, but, when the domestic exchanges are dislocated, the movement of goods between different parts of the country soon comes to a standstill.

When city banks accept bankers' deposits, they incur a heavy responsibility analogous to that of the central banks in Europe. This is particularly true

of the few banks which have acquired the bulk of
the bankers' deposits held by the New York City
banks, partly because of the magnitude of these deposits
but even more on account of the position of New York
as the central money market and clearing house of
the country. The power of outside banks to withdraw money from New York is not limited to their
balances with the banks of the city, since many of
them lend largely there, especially when rates are high.
In emergencies these loans are called, making it necessary for the local banks to shoulder the burden. At
the same time the deposits secured through the payment of these loans give outside banks the right to
withdraw an amount of money largely in excess of
their balances. In responding to demands for cash
secured in this way the New York banks have apparently felt little responsibility and it is in connection
with them that they have taken the first step in restricting payments during successive crises. It should
be remembered, however, that responsibilities are
incurred in return for the profits which accrue to the
New York banks from their central position. London
holds its commanding place because it is known that
money lent there can be instantly recalled. New
York is not meeting the obligations of its position
as our domestic money center, to say nothing of living
up to future international possibilities, so long as it
is unable or unwilling to respond to any demand,
however unreasonable, that can lawfully be made
upon it for cash. This responsibility properly rests
upon the few banks holding bankers' deposits rather
than upon the mass of banks both state and national,

as well as trust companies, whose business is primarily local. The banks with large bankers' balances are in close touch with all parts of the country. It is through them that outside funds are attracted to New York and it is from them that they are withdrawn. The power and profit which these dealings give a few of the New York banks is very great, and it is, therefore, reasonable to expect that they should at all times keep themselves in position to meet any demands which may be made upon them.

While our banks have recognized the necessity of a liberal loan policy in time of crisis, they do not seem to have perceived the equal unwisdom of hoarding their reserves. The national banking law, with its reserve requirements, seems to have blinded our people to the principal purpose and right uses of a reserve. It is not designed to insure a certain percentage of return to depositors in case of failure. A reserve is designed for the use of the many solvent banks in times of emergency, and not for the few insolvent banks. The payment of money to depositors, regardless of what proportion of reserve to liabilities may remain, is the one means which the experience of all countries shows to be effective in allaying panic. In adopting this remedy, the power of issuing notes is advantageous, but not indispensable. It saves the specie reserve from depletion, but in its absence it is only necessary to keep in ordinary times a larger reserve than would otherwise be required.

The panic of 1907 afforded convincing evidence that the fundamental cause of our repeated suspensions of cash payments in time of panic has been the failure of our bankers to adopt any plan of concerted action regarding the use of their reserves. During the last two weeks of October the reserve of the New York banks fell from $265,000,000 to $224,000,-000, and there was then a deficit of $39,000,000 below the 25 per cent. reserve requirement. Thereafter the actual reserve was allowed to decline only $9,000,-000, and during the two remaining months of the year, while a premium was being paid for money, the reserve was even increased to $251,000,000. An illuminating indication of the unsound principles upon which the policy of our banks was based is found in a recent address of the President of the New York clearing-house at the time of the crisis, which is so significant that it may be quoted at some length: —

The Clearing-House Committee knew by experience that the dissipation of the New York banking reserve, upon which practically the credit volume of the nation rests, would alarm the nation, intensify the panic, and greatly prolong the period of recuperation. . . . New York bankers have been severely criticised because they did not more fully respond to the demands of country correspondents by shipping currency against balances. To have fully honored the demands that were pouring in from all sections of the country would have dissipated our banking reserve in a fortnight. How could it be replenished? Were the interior bankers sending currency to New York? What would have been the effect upon the country if the New York banking reserve had been entirely depleted? It would have so intensified the panicky feeling that wide-spread commercial disaster would have resulted. . . . The $53,000,000 deficit in our banking reserve occurred in less than ten days after the failure of the Knickerbocker Trust Company, and was caused by the shipment to interior institutions of the larger portion of that amount in that short time.[1] We kept the door of our treasure house wide open;

[1] As a matter of fact, the reserve deficit was primarily due to the local situation in New York City. On account of the Trust Company situation, the clearing-house

until for the good of the whole country it became necessary to everywhere close it. It never was fully closed; currency shipments continued in a restricted way throughout the panic and a large number of our banks kept up their counter payments as usual.[1]

A contrast with the action taken by the Bank of England at the same time is most striking, and far from flattering to American bankers. At the time of suspension, gold imports had already been engaged, and there was every indication that they would assume large proportions. The Treasury was increasing its deposits with the banks, and a considerable addition to the bank-note circulation was also being made. There was therefore a large addition to our currency in sight. On the other hand, the reserve of the Bank of England at the beginning of the panic was only £24,000,000, and it was reduced after two weeks to £17,000,000, largely through withdrawals for export to the United States. There was not, however, the remotest thought in London that the Bank of England might suspend cash payments, tho the Governor of the Bank of England might have reasoned with perhaps more justification, after the manner of the president of the New York clearing house. The actual amount of money held as reserve in the banking department of the Bank of England, and even in the issue department, was much smaller than

banks increased their loans, and consequently their deposit liabilities, by $70,000,000 during the last two weeks of October. The reported shipments of currency to the interior were more than offset by receipts of government money, so that the net loss of $31,000,000 was unquestionably due to payments in the city itself. — AUTHOR's NOTE.

[1] Commercial and Financial Chronicle, October 10, 1908, Bankers' Convention Section, p. 84.

the reserve of the clearing house banks, and the means for increasing that reserve were by no means more certain.

We seem to have made a sort of fetich of the legal percentage of reserve, giving it an utterly unreal importance as something to be maintained to the sacrifice of every other consideration. We need án elastic reserve policy even more than an elastic currency. The demand for more notes, for purposes which could be directly attained if we would but use our reserves in time of crisis, indicates a misconception of the nature and uses of an elastic currency.

The fact that there are central banks in Europe and a group of reserve-holding banks in New York does not alter in the slightest the nature of the policy to be pursued. The failure to adopt proper methods seems to be due not so much to inability as to a failure to recognize the responsibility of their position by the New York banks which hold bankers' deposits. Local responsibilities are clearly perceived, and properly so, as is indicated by the various money pools organized during the recent panic to provide loans for stock exchange purposes and to assist certain trust companies. Had united action also been taken to meet the demands from outside New York City, it is probable that cash payments would have been generally maintained, and the derangement of the domestic exchanges avoided, with all its accompanying loss to the business community. The difficulties of the situation were in one respect distinctly greater than would present themselves in Europe. It is impossible to make use of personal arguments to convince thousands of country bankers of the unwisdom and inadvisability of some of their demands for money during periods of financial strain. A central bank in this country, however, would be confronted with exactly the same difficulty.

The scramble between the banks to strengthen themselves has been a far more serious element of weakness in all our crises than the withdrawal of funds by individual depositors. Repeated suspensions have created general distrust of the banks among the people and of each other among the banks. The ultimate solvency of the banks is not questioned, but the possibility of securing cash at all times throughout a period of severe financial strain is doubted and with reason. A tradition which is an ever present source of weakness has been established. To break it the banks must successfully endure the strain of a crisis maintaining payments at every point. For this purpose the adoption of legislation which will strengthen the banks generally is not sufficient. We should still be far from certain that the banks would reverse the policy of the past and use all available resources in meeting future emergencies. But if a central bank can be devised which will accomplish precisely this purpose, the utility of measures designed to strengthen the other banks becomes at once apparent. From the point of view, presented in these pages, that a central bank with large lending power will not fit into our system, it is essential that the resources of the existing banks be made adequate or nearly so for all emergency requirements. For this reason I shall first bring forward certain proposals for strengthening our banking system and then present a plan for a central bank of limited scope, the primary purpose of which will be to insure the full use of their resources by the other banks in emergencies.

CHAPTER II

PROPOSALS FOR STRENGTHENING THE EXISTING BANKS

I

THE SEGREGATION OF SAVINGS DEPOSITS

It is my purpose, in this and the chapter following, to analyze further the working of our banking system and to set forth in detail certain modifications in legislation and practice which may be expected to enable the existing banks to serve the community more effectively in normal times and also place them in a better position to meet emergencies. Few of the changes which will be urged are designed exclusively to meet crisis conditions. I shall begin with a proposal the primary purpose of which is to make banking under the national law more profitable, and also more serviceable to the community, tho it will be found to have no little value as a means of strengthening the credit structure. This proposal is the establishment of true savings departments by national banks, the deposits in which shall be segregated and invested under appropriate safeguards.

There is abundant evidence of the urgent need of amending existing legislation if the national banks are to remain the predominant factor in our banking system. For many years credit institutions under state laws, both state banks and trust companies, have been increasing far more rapidly both in number

and in volume of business.[1] A decade or more ago
observers commonly contented themselves with the
explanation that state laws lacked many provisions,
the expression of sound banking principles, which
were to be found in the national law. But this
explanation is no longer even plausible. State banks
and trust companies have steadily, and upon the
whole deservedly, gained in prestige and public confidence. The discredit of a number of the latter in
New York and elsewhere in 1907 served only momentarily to check their growth. Banking under state
laws is certainly more profitable and is also apparently
rendering a more complete and efficient service to
the community than is possible under the national
law. To meet this unsatisfactory situation should
be the first step in legislation, if it can be accomplished
without sacrificing any real element of strength in
the national banking system.

Most of the restrictions in the national banking
law have to do with loans, reserves, or the issue of
notes. Of these the restrictions upon loans are by
far the most serious impediment in competing for
business with state banks and trust companies. For
the banks outside the large cities this is particularly
true of the provision which forbids loans upon real
estate as security.

[1] The following table shows the resources of the three groups of banks at successive ten-year intervals. It probably exaggerates somewhat the growth of state institutions, as the data regarding them secured by the Comptroller of the Currency have
become somewhat more comprehensive in recent years.

Resources of Commercial Banks in the United States [in millions]

	1888	1898	1908
National Banks .	. $2731	$3978	$8714
State Banks .	. 672	1356	4033
Trust Companies	314	942	2866

This restriction is based upon a sound banking principle, learned after much bitter experience. But the experience which led to a complete prohibition of real estate loans was gained amid the economic conditions of the first half of the last century, and the principle itself is one which is applicable only to a particular form of banking organization. While the country was in process of settlement, with an abundance of unoccupied fertile land, real estate was a security of most uncertain value. Moreover, the wildest of the speculative movements which preceded all our early crises were invariably in land. At present, land values are far more stable, and real estate is everywhere included among the most conservative of investments, proper for all with the one exception of commercial banks.

For banks, all of whose obligations are payable upon demand, the real estate loan, quite regardless of its safety, is wisely considered unsuitable. Such loans are commonly wanted by borrowers for a considerable period of time and, therefore, they can not readily be reduced in amount even by an individual bank. In other words, they are not liquid. But the importance of this quality in all its assets disappears when a bank begins to acquire time or savings deposits, as well as those payable on demand. There is, indeed, a strong prejudice in English-speaking countries in favor of the complete division of labor among banking institutions. This view, at no time accepted in other countries, has been steadily losing ground even in Great Britain.[1] In the United States the example

[1] A number of the London joint stock banks have, for example, recently established foreign exchange departments.

of the trust companies shows that a great variety of
financial business can be carried on safely and profitably under a single management. Failures among
them have been comparatively few in number, and
it would be difficult to find a single instance of disaster
which could be attributed to the variety of business
carried on.

Some of the advantages which the banks would
derive if they were able to lend on real estate are so
evident that they require little more than mere men-
tion. It would give them more of the most profitable kind of business, that which has its origin in the
neighborhood of the bank. The immediate return is
generally greater than can be secured from the employment of funds in the money centers or in the purchase
of paper from note brokers. Moreover, in fostering the
growth of wealth and population in its locality a bank
is laying a solid foundation for the future expansion of
its own business. Finally, the ability to lend on real
estate will often enable a bank to secure valuable
customers who would otherwise go elsewhere. It
has been the unpleasant experience of many a national
banker to be obliged to refuse a loan to a would-be
borrower who has nothing but real estate to offer as
security and to see him enter a neighboring state
bank or trust company where there was no legal
obstacle to the transaction. Relations once established are pretty certain to continue even after the
borrower has security which falls within the provisions
of the national law.

There are then at least three distinct advantages
which may be expected to follow if the national banks

are permitted to lend on real estate. It would be profitable for the banks; it would be of advantage to the localities served by the banks; and, finally, it would enable the banks to compete with state institutions upon a more equal footing,[1] thus checking to some extent the relative decline of banking under the national law. All these advantages, and others to be mentioned later, can be secured with no sacrifice of safety by a simple amplification of the existing law. It is only necessary to permit the national banks to establish true savings departments, segregating the deposits, with power to invest them in mortgage loans.

Many of the national banks have already established what are termed savings departments; but they lack most of the essential characteristics of savings institutions. The banks do not have the right to refuse payment on demand; there is no check upon sudden withdrawals aside from the loss incurred by the depositor through payment of interest at half-yearly intervals. Nearly two-fifths of the national banks have established savings departments, the deposits in which amount to $577,000,000, and a large amount in addition has been secured by all the banks in the national system as time deposits including time certificates of deposit. In addition to the reserve requirement, the banks must invest the funds thus secured in accordance with limitations designed to safeguard deposits

---

[1] The importance of real estate to the state banking institutions is shown in the Special Report from the Banks of the United States on April 28, 1909, recently published by the National Monetary Commission. For state banks real estate loans and mortgages amounted to $414,000,000 or 12½ per cent. of total resources and for the trust companies to $377,000,000, more than 9 per cent. of their resources.

the origin and purpose of which is of an entirely different character. No trouble would be experienced if discounts and short-time loans, satisfactory in quality, were to be had in every locality in sufficient quantity to absorb fully the resources of the banks. But these conditions are absent in many parts of the country, especially in those in which agricultural development is the precursor of commercial development.

There are many indications that the local demand for short-time loans is inadequate. Evasions of the law have been frequent and bankers have had the excuse that real estate is often a far better security than that provided by many of their customers whose loans are technically within its requirements. The only alternative has been for banks to employ a part of their resources permanently away from home. No one of the ways open to the banker for this employment is entirely satisfactory.

He may deposit surplus funds in the large cities and secure a beggarly 2 per cent. That this is common practice is shown by the large deposits with reserve agents in excess of the amount serving for reserve purposes. Such deposits, in the case of the country banks, on September 1, 1910, amounted to $437,000,000 of which only $251,000,000 could be counted as a part of the required reserves. In normal times these balances with city banks are a liquid resource, but in emergencies they have invariably proved of very uncertain utility. Between August 22 and December 3, 1907, for example, the country banks were able to reduce their deposits with city banks only from $410,000,000 to $347,000,000. Certainly if the purpose is to maintain themselves in a strong condition the country banks are not well-advised in keeping nearly 10 per cent. of their resources in this form.

Many of the banks regularly hold large investments in securities. On September 1, 1910, these, not including United States bonds, amounted, in the case of the country banks, to $485,000,000, or over 10 per cent. of their total resources. Securities are more satisfactory than balances with city banks as regards the rate of return; they are also a liquid resource in normal times. In emergencies, however, they are an even more unsatisfactory resource than balances with city banks. On account of the inevitable fall in the market price of securities in times of crisis, bankers are unwilling to sacrifice them. Between August and December, 1907, for example, there was a positive increase in such holdings of nearly $22,000,000.

A third alternative is open to the banks: they may lend at a distance, either by the purchase of paper from note brokers or by means of loans on the New York money market. If carefully selected, commercial paper purchased from note brokers is in normal times the most satisfactory investment which a bank can make away from home, both in its rate of return, in liquidness, and in its effect upon the business community. On account of the absence of other relations between borrower and lender, it is a simple matter for the bank to insist upon payment; whereas, in the case of the local borrower, a pretty constant line of credit is commonly expected and secured. It is not, however, to the advantage of the bank to employ any considerable portion of its resources either in purchases of commercial paper or in New York loans. The rate of return is commonly less than that which is secured on local loans, and no valuable permanent relations are established. Moreover, these loans at a distance, like deposits with reserve agents and security holdings, can not be depended upon in emergencies. If the city banks, and particularly those in New York, suspend payments, the country bank is unable to secure the proceeds of its loans because borrowers make payment either in checks or drafts on the city banks.

The portion of the funds of the country banks employed away from home in all these various ways is certainly very great. Any legislation which would tend to increase the amount of purely local business would clearly be of advantage to the banks. That it would also be advantageous to the community is equally certain, and that it would tend to strengthen our banking system in emergencies is highly probable.

In some parts of the eastern states the available supply of capital for all purposes is in excess of local requirements. In such circumstances power to lend on real estate would not be of any particular advantage to the locality. It would simply serve to enable the banks to compete upon a more equal footing with state institutions. Over a far greater part of the country the available supply of bank credit proper, that is, of short-time loans, would also seem to be in excess of local needs, while the opportunities for the use of capital for more permanent objects are by no means exhausted. Here the power to lend on real estate would be of advantage both to the banks and to the community. In the most rapidly advancing sections of the country there would seem to be opportunities for the use of additional amounts of both kinds of loans. Under a highly developed system of branch banking these sections would attract banking credits from other parts of the country, and the country as a whole would thus be making the most effective possible use of this portion of its resources. But under our system of numerous independent local banks there is a very different distribution of credit. Loanable funds move without difficulty from country banks and those of the small cities to the large cities and especially to New York. But the movement goes no further; even tho the demand for loans in its neighborhood is large, the small bank, aside from a moderate amount of temporary accommodation, gets little [1] from the money centers beyond what it has deposited or employed there, and not always all of that. In other words, credit is but imperfectly fluid, or rather, fluid in only one direction. The money centers are reservoirs for the collection from all parts of the country of funds which either temporarily or permanently can not be employed at home, but they are unsatisfactory distributing agents. The banks of the money centers are national in their power to attract money, while in its employment (more especially its regular employment) they are little more than local institutions.

[1] The notes and bills rediscounted, and bills payable, of all the national banks on September 1, 1910, amounted to only $92,600,000, something like 1.7 per cent. of the total loans of the banks, and this amount has seldom been much exceeded.

To some extent, indeed, credit is widely distributed through note brokers. They perform a useful function for large borrowers whose requirements could not be met entirely by the banks of their localities. The note broker brings those whose credit is of the most unquestioned character to the cheapest market for loans; but he does not distribute funds to the localities where they are most needed.

Our practice of depositing reserves in banks of reserve and central reserve cities, and the loans made by banks away from home, do little to equalize the demand and supply of credit between different sections of the country. This failure to make the most advantageous use of available banking credit is, however, a matter of comparatively slight importance. As a result of the widespread habit of using checks there are few parts of the country in which the lack of commercial credit is a serious obstacle to local development. Requirements for capital for prolonged use are in general met far less completely, and on this account any provision which would make possible the employment in this way of a part of the funds that must now be invested in short-time loans, would serve a useful purpose.

Whether under a more perfect system of distribution the existing supply of short-time credit would prove relatively excessive may be left an open question. Under our present system of numerous independent banks there is certainly a wasteful abundance of that form of capital and the disposition which is made of much of it is a serious element of weakness in the credit structure. There is normally in this

country what may be termed a congestion of banking
credit in the money centers and particularly in New
York. The term congestion may seem inapplicable,
inasmuch as the supply of credit in the money centers
is ordinarily fully utilized; but in the case of central
money markets, at any rate, this is a superficial and
even misleading criterion. The demand for short-
time loans for purely industrial purposes is determined
by the volume of business dealings which are being
transacted. It can not be stimulated materially by
the banks even through the offer of low rates, tho,
of course, it may be somewhat enlarged by the acceptance of inferior security. But in the money centers
and particularly in New York the demand for loans
is of a far more expansive nature. Speculative dealings in securities and commodities, and other financial
operations, are capable of almost indefinite growth
if a sufficient amount of credit can be secured. The
volume of speculative dealings on the New York
Stock Exchange is certainly far beyond what is needed
for any useful purpose. It has been very largely
created because of the enormous supply of available
credit furnished by bankers under the wholly
unfounded belief that call loans are always liquid.

The extraordinary amount of credit which is utilized
in these and other financial dealings in New York is
roughly indicated in the reports of the banks of the
city. The total loans of the New York national
banks on April 28, 1909, were $903,000,000; of this
amount $405,500,000 were call loans secured by
collateral, and $225,000,000 were time loans similarly

secured.[1] In the case of the trust companies the total
loans amounted to $595,000,000, of which $251,000,-
000 were call and $266,000,000 were time collateral
loans. Finally, there were $70,000,000 of the former
and $46,000,000 of the latter out of a total of $240,-
000,000 of loans made by the state banks in the city.
For all the New York banks the total of loans was
$1,738,000,000; of this amount $727,000,000, or more
than 40 per cent. were call loans. Including time
collateral loans of $537,000,000, the enormous aggre-
gate of $1,264,000,000, more than 70 per cent. of all
loans, is found to have been based upon stocks,
bonds, and merchandise.[2] No doubt a considerable
portion of these loans was obtained by borrowers for
industrial uses; but, on the other hand, the loans of
outside banks (Canadian as well as American) in the
New York market and those of private lenders and
also finance bills are not included. It would seem
to be fairly certain, therefore, that collateral loans,
approaching in volume those shown by the banks of
the city, were made for financial and speculative
purposes.

Surely it requires no argument to show that the
employment of $1,000,000,000 or more in financial
operations in New York is excessive and wasteful.
Moreover, even if these funds are usefully employed
there would seem to be something radically wrong
in a banking system under which a considerable
portion of them is secured from other parts of the

[1] The collateral loans of the national banks of New York City were 70 per cent.
of all their loans, while those of the banks of the reserve cities, including Chicago and
St. Louis, were less than 40 per cent.

[2] These figures are taken from the Special Report from the Banks of the United
States already referred to.

country where there are abundant opportunities for
the investment of additional capital. Not only are
funds attracted to New York which would otherwise
not be employed but also funds which might serve
to develop local enterprises, if the banks were able
to use a part of their resources in long-time loans on
real estate and other security.

But the absorption of credit in ways which are relatively, if not absolutely, unproductive is not the only,
and it may be added, not the most serious, consequence of this congestion of credit in New York. The
deposit or employment by the banks of a large part
of their resources at a distance is a positive element
of weakness in every emergency. In order to meet
the various business requirements of their customers
the banks necessarily become interdependent, with
various mutual obligations on both sides of the ledger.
In times of crisis there is everywhere the danger,
which is enormously enhanced under a system of
numerous banks, that these relations will be violently
sundered, dislocating the ordinary course of payments
between the banks, their customers, and different
parts of the country. This interdependence of the
banks, tho largely the outgrowth of business convenience and necessity, is, to a very considerable extent, an unnecessary and unhealthy consequence of
legislation designed with quite different objects in
view.

Experience in successive crises has uniformly shown
that the money centers are unable to return any
considerable part of the funds deposited or employed
in them by outside banks. Remedies for this un-

satisfactory situation may be sought in two directions:
if the local banks employed more of their resources
at home the strain on the money centers in emergencies
could not be so severe as it has often been in the past;
on the other hand, if the banks of the money centers
maintained themselves in a stronger position in normal
times they could endure greater strain in times of
difficulty.

The strain upon the money centers in emergencies
may be diminished somewhat by a change in the
national banking law which would permit the banks
to establish savings departments with power to invest
savings deposits in mortgage loans. For the banks
of Wisconsin, for example, to provide a portion of
the funds employed on the New York Stock Exchange
is certainly an uneconomic use of their resources if
there are opportunities for investment at home on
real security; and it is doubly undesirable because
it tends to weaken the entire credit structure. The
national banks of that state already hold nearly
$27,000,000 in savings deposits and doubtless this
amount could be largely increased. At present the
deposits of the Wisconsin banks with reserve agents
are nearly $5,500,000 more than are available for
reserve purposes, an excess of over 75 per cent.
Whether the Wisconsin banks are also lending to any
considerable extent outside the state can not be
determined, tho it is highly probable.

The extent to which real estate loans would enable
the banks to dispense with the employment of funds
at a distance is uncertain. It is not to be supposed
that this power alone would be sufficient to remove

this element of weakness. But even if it serve only to check somewhat the tendency to employ funds at a distance it would at least diminish the strain of future emergencies.

The ability of the national banks to attract savings deposits is evident. Even in New England, where the field would seem to be fully occupied by savings banks and trust companies, one hundred and nineteen of the four hundred and seventy-four national banks have opened savings departments and have secured deposits amounting to more than $39,000,000. In the Western and Southern states, in which savings institutions under state laws are comparatively few, much larger results are to be expected from a national savings bank law.

The urgent need of generally diffused facilities for savings has recently led to the establishment of a postal savings bank system. A national savings bank law would, however, permit of a very wide extension of such facilities. If the banks were permitted to open agencies for the receipt and payment of savings deposits in every place in their immediate neighborhood in which there is no national bank and upon condition that such agencies be withdrawn upon the establishment of a bank, savings facilities could be almost as widely diffused as under a postal system. In most other respects, the superior advantages of national savings banks are clear and unquestioned. The accumulation of capital is far greater in some sections of the country than in others. Presumably postal savings banks will attract depositors most largely in those sections of the country in which savings facilities are now lacking. They are just those sections in which there are the most abundant opportunities for further investment. The deposits in the postal savings banks will be invested in government bonds and possibly in the bonds of the states and of municipalities. To draw money away from Idaho or Oklahoma, for example, for such investments is unwise. It will be taking money from parts of the country where interest rates are high to place it in investments yielding a low rate of return, a rate determined by the accumulation of investment funds in the eastern money centers. Savings will be taken from parts of the country in which the rate of interest is high, simply because of the attractive facilities for savings furnished by the government.[1] Can it be questioned that the development of the country will be better served by the employment of savings by the individual banks in fostering the development of their own localities ?

In formulating a national savings bank law the codes of a number of the eastern states would serve as admirable models, but the opportunity should not be lost of taking one important step forward in such legislation. The banks should be protected against their savings depositors far more completely than has been customary in the practice of state savings institutions. Savings depositors seem somewhat

---

[1] The postal savings law will almost certainly tend to increase the employment of their resources by the banks away from home. Under the provisions of the act, deposits, received at the several post offices, are to be turned over to the local banks, but as they are to be payable on demand and safeguarded by the deposit of securities supported by the taxing power, they will not be available for mortgage loans, but only at best for those local purposes for which it is already most easy to secure distant capital.

more liable to spasms of unreasoning fear than the business depositors of commercial banks. In many of the states, savings banks are empowered to require notice of the withdrawal of deposits, and have made use of the power in every period of crisis. But it is a power which is not well understood by the mass of depositors and its exercise has therefore probably done quite as much harm as good. Many depositors look upon the step as an indication of insolvency and refrain from making their customary weekly and monthly additions to their savings accounts. Money is hoarded which in normal times passes from wage-earners into circulation through the channel of the savings banks. This has been an important influence responsible for the dearth of currency which has characterized our successive crises. Savings depositors should be made to understand that the withdrawal of their deposits without notice is a matter of favor. It might be well if a week's notice were regularly required for the withdrawal of any amount exceeding $25, a sum ample to meet urgent needs of the ordinary savings depositor. Then the longer notice exacted in emergencies would excite less alarm. The more widely savings institutions are established the more necessary will it become to impress upon depositors the nature of the obligations and investments of the savings bank. State institutions can not be controlled in this matter, but it is to be expected that the expression of this sound principle in national legislation would have a potent influence upon them.

II

A PLAN FOR STRENGTHENING RESERVES

We shall now turn our attention to a change in our
banking system designed primarily to enable the
banks to cope more successfully with crisis conditions.
For this purpose it is fortunately not necessary to
impose additional burdensome restrictions upon the
conduct of the daily operations of the banks. The
adoption of such remedies would diminish the profits
of the banks and their power to serve the business
community, and would also make it even more difficult than at present to compete with state credit
institutions. With the exception of 1893, none of
our crises has disclosed among any considerable
number of the national banks a condition of weakness
so extreme as to involve impairment of capital, much
less insolvency.[1]

In each of our successive crises the same defects
in our banking system have been made manifest.
They have been the result not of unsound methods
of handling the individual banks but of the imperfect
organization of the system. At no time, except
during periods of acute trade depression, have the
banks been in a position to withstand severe strain.
Nowhere has there been adequate reserve power to
meet emergencies by means of the expansion of loans
and the payment of cash in sufficient amount to allay
the alarm of depositors. At the outbreak of the

[1] The bank failures of 1893 were largely in the West and Southwest, where economic
conditions were so generally unsound that no conceivable restrictions could have
shielded the banks from serious trouble.

crises of 1873 and 1893 the banks were not appreciably
less well supplied with cash resources than in the years
immediately preceding; and in 1907 the ratio of this
part of their reserve to deposit liabilities was considerably above what it had been during a number of the
years since the beginning of the century.[1] To require
by legislation that all the banks shall have adequate
power in reserve for emergencies would be a difficult,
even an impossible, undertaking, to say nothing of
the burden of expense which it would place upon the
banks and consequently upon the community. Proposals for an asset currency, which seem to be designed
to bring this about in a less expensive fashion, have
failed to secure general favor, largely, it may be
surmised, because of the widespread feeling that the
banks would exhaust this as they have their other
credit resources before an emergency came upon
them.

Fortunately a less diffused reserve power is sufficient for the purpose and can be secured by means
of more simple and less hazardous arrangements. It
is only necessary to insure the maintenance of this
power in reserve where the strain of crises is most
severe and to make certain that it will be put to use.
This is accomplished in most other countries entirely
through central banks; and were it not for political
and economic difficulties, in particular the absence of
branch banking, the same result doubtless might be
achieved in this country. Other means can be devised, however, which would probably prove adequate,

[1] In regard to this and other statements of fact regarding our crises the reader is
referred to a History of the National Banks during Crises by the writer, one of the
publications of the National Monetary Commission.

and which would also pave the way for the establishment of a central bank of limited scope which will fit into our peculiar banking organization.

In every country there is a central money market to which is always shifted nearly the entire burden of supporting the credit structure in emergencies. This is obvious in any country in which banking is carried on by a few banks with many branches, since the central offices of such banks are with few exceptions in its chief money center. In the United States with its multitude of independent local banks it is, indeed, less obvious, but it is no less certain that this burden rests upon the central money market of the country, New York City. Some of our crises and panics, like those of 1884 and 1907, began in New York. Others began elsewhere, as, for example, the crisis of 1893, which set in with failures in the West and South. But in all cases the consequent strain was immediately felt in New York with no apparent diminution in violence.

The significance of the New York money market in our banking system is not fully recognized. It is indeed generally understood that the practice of depositing reserves with agents in the money centers places a severe strain upon them in emergencies, and it is well known that the New York banks have acquired a large share of such deposits. The enormous responsibilities resting upon the New York banks on this account will be seen in the following table, which shows the distribution of bankers' deposits among the national banks on September 1, 1909: —

	New York	Chicago and St. Louis	Forty-six Reserve Cities
Number of Banks	38	23	321
Due to National Banks [1] .	$331	$198	$381
Due to Other Banks . . .	346	110	403
Total Bankers' Deposits .	677	308	784
Due from National Banks	49	76	167
Due from Other Banks . .	9	17	60
Net Bankers' Deposits . .	619	215	557
Due from Reserve Agents	——	——	266

The New York banks held about one-third of the total amount of bankers' deposits; and if the more significant obligation of net bankers' deposits is taken, they held more than 43 per cent. of the total. Compared with the banks of Chicago and St. Louis their obligations to bankers were almost three times as great.

And this is not all. From the table it will be observed that the amount due to the banks of Chicago and St. Louis from other national banks was $76,000,-000, while in the case of the New York banks it was only $49,000,000. But the total resources of the New York banks are about two and one-half times as large as those of the Chicago and St. Louis banks. A large portion of the amount due to the banks of the two western central reserve cities consists of balances with the New York banks. This is well known, tho no figures of the exact amount of such balances are available. Large New York balances are necessary because New York is the clearing house of the country. In this connection certain statistics [2] gathered by the Comptroller of the Currency nearly

[1] These and the following items in millions.
[2] See Report of the Comptroller of the Currency, 1891, pp.16–23.

twenty years ago have great significance. From information provided by 3,329 of the 3,438 national banks it was found that in 1890 all but three drew drafts upon New York and that the total amount of such drafts was 61.31 per cent. of all the drafts drawn upon all the banks of the country. In the case of the Chicago banks the amount drawn was but 9.82 per cent. of the total. The Chicago banks drew upon New York for $222,000,000 and were drawn upon in return for but $82,000. These figures show very clearly how indispensable is the maintenance of payments by the New York banks if the dislocation of the domestic exchanges is to be avoided. If every bank throughout the country were required to keep its entire reserve in its own vaults the likelihood of suspension in New York would be diminished, but general suspension would be no less certain to follow if that step were taken by the New York banks.

The strain upon the New York banks in emergencies is not limited to the withdrawals of balances by outside banks. Like the central money markets of other countries, New York is the cheapest market for loans in the United States and is consequently resorted to by large borrowers from all sections. For this reason and on account of stock exchange and other financial dealings the demand for loans there is indefinitely large and attracts the surplus funds of the banks of the entire country. Loans of outside banks in New York are apt to be particularly large during those periods of months or even years when conditions are ripening for a crisis, because at such times the rates for loans in money centers always reach abnormally high levels. When a crisis does come, calls from the outside banks for the liquidation of their loans and the shipment of the currency received in payment are invariably even more in evidence than the drawing down of balances. The effects are far more disturbing because of the shifting of loans which is involved.[1]

There has been no crisis since the establishment of the national banking system in which the New York banks would have been at all likely to have resorted to suspension had their difficulties been confined to those of purely local origin. In 1873 the situation in New York was so far improved at the time the banks restricted payments that the necessity for it was generally questioned. It was subsequently explained in a clearing house committee report that the measure was taken on account of the threatened exhaustion of the cash reserves of the banks in response to the demands of the interior banks for the return of their deposits.[2] In 1893 there was nothing in the nature of a panic in New York itself, when this discreditable step was again taken. The banks succumbed to the prolonged drain of money to the West and Southwest, where numerous bank failures had generally weakened public confidence. Again, in the crisis of 1907, at the end of the week in which the troubles of the New York trust companies became

[1] Since the appearance of outside banks as large lenders in the New York money market it has been no longer possible for the clearing house banks to reduce their loans in emergencies. During the last two weeks of October and the first week of November, 1907, the loans of the latter were increased by over $110,000,000.

[2] This illuminating report should be better known. It will be found in the Commercial and Financial Chronicle, November 15, 1873, and in the Bankers' Magazine, December, 1873; also in my History of Crises, pp. 91–103.

known, the local situation was showing such decided evidence of improvement that but for the increased demands of the outside banks it is certain that cash payments would have been maintained. The course of events in all these crises shows plainly the source of weakness in our banking system and the general nature of the remedies which should be adopted. The burden resting upon the New York banks should, if possible, be lightened and, above all, their ability to endure severe strain should be increased.

Something can be accomplished in the way of diminishing the responsibilities of the New York banks in emergencies; tho perhaps not much, since these responsibilities are an inevitable consequence of the position of the city as the clearing house and money center of the country. We have already seen that the investment of savings deposits in long-time loans may be expected to check somewhat the flow of money to New York. This is especially probable in the case of banks in those parts of the West and South where there are still abundant opportunities for the further investment of capital. As it has been precisely from banks of these sections that the demand upon New York in emergencies has been most urgent, the effect of their partial withdrawal from the New York market would probably be much greater than might be expected, judging solely from the relative magnitude of the funds thus employed.

Something also may be accomplished toward reducing the strain upon New York by a modification of the reserve requirements of the national banking law. The present arrangement with its three classes of banks, or rather of localities, has nothing to recommend it. It has failed whenever it has been subjected to severe test. No bank which holds large bankers' deposits, particularly when these form a part of the reserves of other banks, should be permitted to keep its own reserve anywhere except in its own vaults. There are a number of banks in the reserve cities each of which has acquired upwards of $15,000,000 of bankers' deposits. For these banks to be allowed to keep half of their reserves with central reserve city banks is an arrangement based neither upon business convenience nor sound principle. It places virtually the entire burden of supporting the credit structure upon the banks of central reserve cities which hold bankers' deposits. Moreover, on account of the deposits and funds employed in New York by the banks of Chicago and St. Louis, this burden rests almost entirely upon the few banks in that city which hold the lion's share of the deposits of other banks.

This unsatisfactory situation can be remedied, in some measure, by a simple change in the present law. It would only be necessary to impose the requirement of a 25 per cent. cash reserve upon any bank wherever situated which should choose to qualify as a reserve agent for other banks. It might also be advisable to limit this power to banks in places with a certain minimum population and with a minimum of capital (which might be placed as high as $500,000 or even $1,000,000). Under this arrangement the distinction between reserve and central reserve cities would disappear. There would be but two classes of banks: local banks which might be established anywhere, and reserve agent banks which might be established in any place having the required minimum population.

It is impossible to formulate any legislation regarding reserve requirements which will be entirely satisfactory. The responsibilities of banks in different localities are not entirely similar, and the responsibilities of the various banks in any one locality are even more diverse. The present law over-emphasizes the importance of differences in localities and even then does not accomplish the end in view. The banks in a city which is a commercial and financial center for the region about it have responsibilities which exceed those of the banks of a city whose business is of a purely local nature. But this difference can not be determined by the test of population. In those parts of the country in which the population is dense the banks in a city with a comparatively large number of inhabitants may be of little more than local importance. On the other hand, in the agricultural West and South, important centers for commercial and banking business may have a very small population. Aside from a minimum population requirement, the present law leaves to the banks the determination of the rank of each place. The results have been not a little curious. The banks of some important cities like Buffalo, Atlanta, and Memphis have elected to remain country banks. In the Western States, where the rivalry of cities is keen, reserve cities are more numerous. Texas already has six and the state of Washington three.

Under the proposed arrangement opportunity would be given to many individual banks, at scattered points throughout the country, to develop a business which would be profitable to themselves and of service to their localities. The deposited reserves of the country banks would probably not then be found so frequently in a city distant hundreds or even thousands of miles. This was a cause of the temporary suspension of many banks in 1893, and similar mishaps would doubtless have occurred in 1907 if general suspension had not come almost at the very beginning of that crisis. Under the proposed arrangement, further, the heavy responsibility which rests upon those banks which hold bankers' deposits would be more apparent to the general public than it is at present. At the same time it would relieve many banks of a burden which is also a serious obstacle to the growth of banking under the national law in reserve cities. By no means all the banks in the reserve cities have acquired bankers' deposits. Many of them are engaged in purely local business and do not need larger reserves than local banks elsewhere. Certainly if the present requirement is sufficient for the country banks of Buffalo and Atlanta, it would be adequate for the purely local banks of Boston or San Francisco. That the present arrangement is a serious obstacle to the growth of the national system in reserve cities is certain. With the exception of a few cities in which many national banks were formed after the Civil War, the number of national banks in reserve cities is exceedingly small. There are at present forty-six reserve cities; in three of these (Savannah, Topeka, and Tacoma) there are only two national banks; in seven there are only three; and in nine there are only four national banks. In most instances a national charter is secured only when the organizers of the bank intend to compete for bankers' deposits. Banks designed for purely local business are organized under state laws.

The effect of the proposed change upon the cash reserves of the banks can not, of course, be determined exactly. It would certainly increase somewhat the required cash holdings of the national banks, taken as a whole, against a given net deposit liability. On September 1, 1909, the three hundred and twelve banks in reserve cities held a cash reserve, including the 5 per cent. fund, of $231,800,000, or 13.5 per cent. of their net deposits. Nearly $200,000,000 in addition would be required if all the banks were to qualify as reserve agents. But it is certain that by no means all of them would qualify, since many of them have little or no bankers' deposits. It would seem to be a safe assumption that not more than two-thirds of the total deposit liability of these banks would belong to banks which would become reserve agents. Upon this assumption not more than $133,000,000 would be needed. The withdrawal of this sum from the banks in the central reserve cities, by reducing their deposit liabilities, would set free $33,000,000 now held as reserve. It would seem safe, therefore, to assume that about $100,000,000 would be required to carry out this change. This is an amount not much greater than the trust companies of New York City were obliged to accumulate in consequence of state legislation passed after the crisis of 1907. If provision were made for compliance with this requirement over a period of two or three years, it could certainly be carried through with no seriously disturbing consequences.[1]

This estimate of the amount of money required to provide all banks holding bankers' deposits with a 25 per cent. cash reserve would be still further reduced if the banks of the present reserve cities engaged in purely local business were to be assimilated to the country banks for reserve purposes. Moreover, some change in the reserve of most of the country banks would follow the establishment of true savings departments. The present reserve requirement is too high for savings deposits the withdrawal of which is properly safeguarded. The opportunity would, therefore, be provided to increase the cash reserve against deposits payable on demand without imposing an additional burden upon any considerable number of the country banks. The requirement of a cash reserve of 10 per cent and a deposited reserve of 5 or even 10 per cent would involve little or no addition

[1] Mr. Victor Morawetz has brought forward, in his suggestive volume entitled The Banking and Currency Problem in the United States [second edition, pp. 122–129] a plan for a more thoro-going reconstruction of our reserve system. He proposes a uniform reserve requirement against ordinary deposits for all the banks of the country and a much higher requirement against bankers' deposits. There would be no deposited reserves, so far as the law is concerned. Purely for illustrative purposes, he suggests 10 per cent. against ordinary deposits and 30 per cent. against bankers' deposits. The 10 per cent. requirement would involve the moderate increase of $40,000,000 in the cash reserves of the country banks, and would, of course, reduce the requirement for banks in reserve and central reserve cities. The 30 per cent. requirement against bankers' deposits would be clearly insufficient. With the possible exception of a very few banks in reserve cities total cash requirements would be less than under the present law and very much less in the case of central reserve city banks. It would be necessary to have a reserve of something like 50 per cent. against bankers' deposits in order to strengthen materially the banks of the money centers. The proposal in the text involves far less departure from our existing arrangements and its effects can therefore be more definitely predicted. The purpose of the two proposals is not essentially different.

either to their present stock of money or to the amount
of their deposits with reserve agents. It would simply
insure retention of the existing reserve after the con-
version of demand deposits into savings deposits.

This scheme of requirements, it is submitted, is
adjusted to the varying responsibilities of the banks
as nearly as is possible under legislative provisions
which are necessarily more or less rigid in character.
It does fail to meet the special responsibilities which
rest upon banks in the money centers of the first
rank, even tho their business is purely local. The
failure of purely local banks in New York may have
wide consequence if it disturbs confidence in those
banks of the city whose business relations are national
in scope. This, however, is an aspect of the situation
which would diminish in importance under the proposed arrangement because it emphasizes the responsibilities of banks not by localities but with reference
to their position as reserve agents. Finally, it may
be observed that in the great cities the banks themselves may be relied upon to insure the maintenance
of proper standards through the clearing house.
Some years before the establishment of the national
banking system the New York Clearing House Association adopted the rule requiring a 25 per cent cash
reserve, and this rule would doubtless be continued
even tho the present law were to be changed.

III

THE RELATION BETWEEN CLEARING HOUSE LOAN CERTIFICATES AND SUSPENSION

Up to this point we have been considering means of diminishing the strain upon the New York banks through changes which would directly affect the other banks. By means of savings departments a considerable amount of demand deposits would be converted into time deposits and a greater part of the funds of the banks would be employed at home. The proposed change in reserve requirements would increase somewhat the ratio of the cash reserve to demand deposits without imposing any appreciable burden upon the banks, and would largely increase the cash reserve of those banks outside the present central reserve cities which hold bankers' deposits. These banks, like those of Chicago and St. Louis, would doubtless carry considerable balances in New York and also employ surplus funds in that market; but their withdrawals of funds from it in emergencies could hardly reach the proportions possible under the present system.

All these various arrangements would avail little, however, if the banks in future emergencies make no more use of their reserves than they did in 1893 or 1907. On those occasions the New York banks resorted to suspension long before their reserves were exhausted. While the power of outside banks to deplete the reserves of the New York banks may be somewhat curtailed, some means for insuring the

effective use of reserves is absolutely essential if we
are to escape suspension in future emergencies.

Since the establishment of the national banking
system suspension, more or less complete, has been
resorted to on three occasions, — in 1873, in 1893,
and in 1907. On all these occasions the country
banks had increased their cash reserves and the ratio
of their reserves to deposit liabilities during the
interval between the outbreak of the disturbance
and suspension. The banks of the reserve cities and
also those of Chicago and St. Louis, while experiencing
some loss in their cash holdings managed to maintain
their reserve ratio with almost no change. The
showing of the New York banks has been in every instance somewhat more creditable, since they have lost
heavily in cash, and their reserve ratio has gone below
the 25 per cent. requirement. In the case of the
other banks, however, it should be remembered that
in suspending payments they were simply following
in the wake of the New York banks. When the New
York banks suspend, similar action is inevitable elsewhere, at least for all banks whose customers have
wide business dealings, because through New York
payments are made between different parts of the
country. Moreover, there is no reason to believe
that the country banks were intending to hoard the
money which they withdrew from their reserve agents
at the beginning of each of our successive crises. They
needed additional supplies of cash if they were to
meet the demands of their own depositors. But
after the New York banks suspended the country
banks naturally held with a tight grip all the money

which they had in their possession and also endeavored to extract more from their reserve agents. The fact that the country banks held more cash in December than in August, 1907, is no indication whatever of what their position would have been if the banks in New York had not inaugurated the policy of suspension. Surely it can not be held that the country banks should not withdraw any money from their reserve agents in emergencies. And after suspension the country banks in holding their reserves intact were following a course exactly similar to that of the city banks. The New Yorks banks themselves in 1907 held a larger reserve at the beginning of December than at the beginning of the previous month.

One of the unfortunate effects of suspension is the creation of seemingly conclusive evidence for its necessity. During the last two months of 1907 cash payments were generally restricted by the banks and, altho an enormous amount of money was added to the supply in the country, none of it was secured by the banks. Through gold imports, government deposits, issues of banknotes, and payments of cash by the banks, something like $300,000,000 was added to the amount of money in every-day use or in hoards. Furthermore, a vast amount of substitutes for money was set afloat in the community.[1] It has been assumed that as much as this amount of money, perhaps more, would have been taken from the banks if they had not restricted payments. This view is, however, contrary to experience in every instance where banks

[1] See the careful estimate by Professor A. P. Andrew, in the Quarterly Journal of Economics, August, 1908.

have met the demands of depositors fearlessly in an
emergency. Suspension increases enormously the
propensity to hoard money; it also makes more
sluggish the movement of money which is in actual
use. We can not be absolutely certain that the New
York banks would have been able to maintain payments until calm was restored; but the amount of
money which went out of sight after suspension is no
indication whatever of the amount which would
have been required to maintain cash payments.

Comparison of the course of events during the
crisis of 1873 with that in subsequent crises shows a
progressively increasing unwillingness or inability
among the New York banks to make use of their cash
reserves. In 1873 the New York banks at the outset
of the crisis held an available reserve of $34,300,000.
In the course of four weeks this was reduced to
$5,800,000, and the ratio to deposit liabilities was
then less than 4.5 per cent.[1] Suspension was not
escaped in 1873 but it was of shorter duration than
in later crises. The banks at that time were unable
to increase their cash resources by any of the means
which have been available in later crises. The government had no surplus of greenbacks, aside from about
$12,000,000 which was almost entirely secured and
retained by the savings banks. Banknotes could
not be issued because the total circulation was at
that time limited by law. Finally, additional supplies

[1] The figures in the text refer to the legal tender holdings of the banks. The banks
also held a considerable amount of specie but it was not a free asset, as most of it had
been received on special accounts payable in gold. Including the specie holdings the
reserve ratio was 12.8 per cent.

of gold, secured through imports, were useless for ordinary banking purposes because the business of the country was then carried on by means of an inconvertible and depreciated paper currency. Notwithstanding all these special difficulties, the New York banks, by continuing to use their reserves freely even after payments had been restricted, were able to restore confidence in a comparatively short time, and money began to flow back to them within three weeks after the outbreak of the crisis.

In 1893 the New York banks were in what was for them an unusually strong condition at the beginning of the disturbance, having early in June a cash reserve exceeding 30 per cent of their net deposits. A succession of banking failures in the West and South led to heavy withdrawals from New York during the latter part of June and the beginning of July. Then followed a lull and money began to be returned to New York. During the third week of July banking failures were renewed in the West and South and the drain was resumed. The positively unfavorable aspects of the situation were altogether similar to those of the previous month with the one further circumstance of a reduced cash reserve in New York. On the other hand, additional means with which to meet the situation were becoming available. At the end of July gold imports in large amount had been arranged. Foreign purchases of our securities were heavy, reflecting increasing confidence in the repeal of the silver purchase law. Arrangements had also been made which would certainly lead to a considerable increase in the issues of banknotes during August and September. Notwithstanding all these favorable circumstances the New York banks suspended, during the first week of August, when they still held a cash reserve of $79,000,000, more than 20 per cent of their deposit liabilities.

In 1907 the New York banks restricted payments when they still held a cash reserve of more than $220,000,000 and when the reserve ratio was also above 20 per cent. Both in 1893 and in 1907 suspension was not a measure of last resort taken after the banks had entirely exhausted their reserves and when there were no means of securing additional cash resources. Moreover, after cash payments were restricted the policy of the banks was unlike that adopted in 1873, in that the banks did not make further use of their reserves; they hoarded them and added to their amount, thus unduly prolonging the period of suspension.

Explanation of the failure of the banks in 1893 and 1907 to use their cash resources as completely as in 1873 is simple; but it is of the very greatest significance because it will bring to light the most serious element of weakness in our credit structure.

In 1893 and in 1907 the clearing house loan certificate was the only device resorted to in order to secure the adoption of a common policy by the banks. In 1873, as on earlier occasions when its use was authorized, provision was also made for the equalization of the reserves of the banks. Thus in 1873 the Clearing House Association in addition to the customary arrangements for the issue of loan certificates adopted the following resolution: —

That in order to accomplish the purposes set forth in this agreement the legal tenders belonging to the associated banks shall be considered and treated as a common fund, held for mutual aid and protection, and the committee appointed shall have power to equalize the same by assessment or otherwise at their discretion. For this purpose a statement shall be made to the committee of the condition of such bank on the morning of every day, before the opening of business, which shall be sent with the exchanges to the manager of the Clearing House, specifying the following items: —

(1) Loans and discounts. (2) Amount of loan certificates. (3) Amount of United States certificates of deposit and legal tender notes. (4) Amount of deposits deducting therefrom the amount of special gold deposits.

Two fairly distinct powers were given the clearing house committee: the right to issue clearing house certificates, and control over the currency portion of the reserves of the banks. This machinery was devised (according to tradition) after the crisis of 1857 by George S. Coe, who for more than thirty years was President of the American Exchange National Bank. The purpose of the certificate was to remove certain serious difficulties which had become generally recognized during that crisis. The banks had pursued a policy of loan contraction which ultimately led to general suspension, because it had proved impossible to secure any agreement among them.[1] The banks which were prepared to assist the business community with loans could not do so because they would be certain to be found with unfavorable clearing-house balances in favor of the banks which followed a more selfish course. The loan certificate provided a means of payment other than cash. What

[1] C. F. Dunbar, Economic Essays, chap. xvi.

was more important, it took away the temptation
from any single bank to seek to strengthen itself at
the expense of its fellows, and rendered each bank
more willing to assist the community with loans to the
extent of its power.

But in addition to the arrangement for the use of
loan certificates provision was also made for what was
called the equalization of reserves. The individual
banks were not of course equally strong in reserves
at the times when loan certificates were authorized.
From that moment they would be unable to strengthen
themselves, aside from the receipt of money from
depositors, except in so far as the other banks should
choose to meet unfavorable balances in cash. Moreover, withdrawals of cash by depositors would not
fall evenly upon the banks. Some would find their
reserves falling away rapidly with no adequate means
of replenishing them. The enforced suspension of
individual banks would pretty certainly involve the
other banks in its train. Finally, it would not be
impossible for a bank to induce friendly depositors to
present checks on other banks directly for cash payment, instead of depositing them for collection and
probable payment in loan certificates, through the
clearing house. The arrangement for equalizing
reserves therefore diminished the likelihood of the
banks working at cross purposes — a danger which
the use of clearing house certificates alone can not
entirely remove.

These arrangements had enabled the banks to pass
through periods of severe strain in 1860 and in 1861

without suspension. In both instances the use of the loan certificate was followed immediately by an increase in the loans of the banks, and in no short time by an increase in their reserves. The situation in 1873 was more serious, and as events proved, the reserve strength of the banks, while sufficient to carry them through the worst of the storm, was not enough to enable them to avoid the resort to suspension.

In 1884, the next occasion when clearing house loan certificates were issued, the opposition to the provision for the equalization of reserves was so widespread that it does not appear that it was even formally considered. The ground for this opposition can be readily understood. In 1873 the practice of paying interest upon bankers' deposits was generally regarded with disfavor. Only twelve of the clearing house banks offered this inducement to attract deposits; but by this means they had secured the bulk of the balances of outside banks. It was in meeting the requirements of these banks that the reserves of all the banks were exhausted at that time. The non-interest paying banks entered into the arrangement for the equalization of reserves in expectation of securing a clearing house rule against the practice of paying interest on deposits. But their efforts had resulted in failure. Some of them had employed their reserves for the common good most reluctantly in 1873, and the feeling against a similar arrangement in 1884 was naturally far stronger and more general. Moreover, the working of the pooling agreement in 1873 had occasioned heart-burnings which had not entirely disappeared with the lapse of time. It was believed,

and doubtless with reason, that some of the banks
had evaded the obligations of the pooling agreement.
It was said that some of the banks had encouraged
special currency deposits so as not to be obliged to
turn money into the common fund. Further, as the
arrangement had not included banknotes, banks
exchanged greenbacks for notes in order either to
increase their holdings of cash or to secure money
for payment over the counter. Here we come upon
an objection to the pooling arrangement which doubtless had much weight with the specially strong banks,
altho it is more apparent than real. In order to
supply the pressing requirements of some banks,
others who believed that they would have been able
to meet all the demands of their depositors were
obliged to restrict payments. That such an expectation would have proved illusory later experience
affords ample proof. When a large number of the
banks in any locality suspend, the others can not
escape adopting the same course. But in 1884 the
erroneousness of the belief had not been made clear
by recent experience.

The New York banks weathered the moderate
storms of 1884 and 1890 without suspension, by means
of the clearing house loan certificate alone, and in
the course of time all recollection of the arrangement
for the equalization of reserves seems to have faded
from the memory of the banking community. There
was, however, in those years another potent influence
which tended to lessen the likelihood of suspension
following the issue of loan certificates. Many banks
were unwilling to take them out, fearing that such

action would be regarded as a confession of weakness. The prejudice against them was indeed so strong that needed loan expansion did not follow the authorization of their issue. In 1890 the directors of the Bank of Commerce, then, as now, one of the most important banks of the city, passed a resolution urging other banks to relieve the situation by increasing loans and by taking out loan certificates.

In 1893 only a small part of the balances between the banks was settled in certificates at first; but by the end of July practically all balances were settled in that way and suspension followed at once. In 1907 all the banks having unfavorable balances, with but one important exception, took out certificates on the first day that their issue was authorized, and suspension was then for the first time simultaneous with their issue.

The connection between suspension and the use of clearing house loan certificates as the sole medium of payment between the banks is simple and direct. The bank which receives a relatively large amount of drafts and checks on other banks from its customers can not pay out cash indefinitely if it is unable to secure any money from the banks on which they are drawn. So long as only a few banks are taking out certificates and the bulk of payments are made in money, no difficulty is experienced; but as soon as all the banks make use of that medium, the suspension of the banks which have large numbers of correspondents soon becomes inevitable. The contention of bankers both in 1893 and in 1907 that they had not suspended since they had only refused to honor drafts on other banks was untenable. The clearing house loan certificate was a device which the banks themselves had adopted and they had failed to provide any means for preventing partial suspension as the result of its use. The further contention of some bankers that they had suspended because they had no money to pay out was doubtless true of a few banks, but for that very reason other banks must have been all the stronger, probably well above their required reserve.

That the arrangement for equalizing the reserves, adopted in 1873, would have availed to prevent suspension on subsequent occasions, is highly probable, indeed a practical certainty. In 1893 events proved that the banks had maintained payments up to the very last of the succession of disasters with the results of which they had been contending. During August the number of bank failures was not large and none of them was of great importance. We can not, of course, know how soon money would have begun to flow back to New York, but certainly the suspension of payments could hardly have hastened the movement. From the beginning of September the reported movements of currency showed a gain for the New York banks, and for the week ending September 16 the gain was no less than $8,000,000. One month more of drain, therefore, was the most that the banks would have been obliged to endure, and for the needs of that month the banks would not, as in 1873, have been confined to the single resource of the $79,000,000 of the cash in their vaults.[1]

---

[1] The increase in the amount of money in circulation for August, 1893, was estimated at $70,000,000.

Similarly, the enormous increase in the money supply of the country in November and December, 1907, would have offset much of the loss of reserve which the banks would have incurred, if they had continued to meet all the demands of their customers for cash. And, finally, it may be observed that in the unlikely event that alarm had not been allayed and suspension in the end had become unavoidable, it would not have made any practical difference to depositors whether the reserves of the banks had been but 10 per cent. rather than 20 per cent. of their demand liabilities.

The probability that the equalization of reserves would have served to prevent suspension in 1893 and also in 1907, brings up the question whether the banks may reasonably be expected to resort to the arrangement in an emergency. At first sight it seems unreasonable to expect banks which reap no advantage from bankers' deposits to employ their reserves to meet needs with which they are not directly concerned. On the other hand, all the banks agree upon, and share in the use of, the clearing house loan certificate. It is a device which enables the banks to meet the demand for loans, and as the loans of the New York banks are principally to local borrowers it is the local situation that is thus relieved. This is the proper policy for banks in any locality. But it should not be carried out at the cost of the rest of the community or be allowed to overshadow all other responsibilities. The continuance of loans enables the banks to escape almost inevitable loss from failures of customers through the sudden contraction of credit, and also

enables them to earn profits for their share-holders.
Individually all the New York banks reap an advantage not only from the clearing house loan certificate
but also from the position of New York as the money
center of the country; and anything which under-
mines its reputation for strength is harmful to all.
Finally, profits are not sacrificed when reserves are
equalized, as the reserve is not a source of profit; it
is a foundation of credit, and a resource for emergencies.
The use of a reserve does not in any way reduce the
gains of a bank from its loans or other profitable
operations. The objection to equalization is the
natural objection to assisting those who should have
assisted themselves; it rests upon a sound basis of
human experience; but it does not follow that the
refusal to co-operate must be absolute. It may be
conditional upon amendment. This was the attitude
of the more conservative banks in 1873. As often
happens, their hopes of amendment were not realized.
They proposed an indirect remedy, the prohibition
of the payment of interest on bankers' deposits. A
more direct remedy would be secured through the
insistence by clearing house authorities and the public
that banks holding these highly explosive bankers'
deposits should hold larger reserves in normal times
than are held by the banks carrying on a purely local
business.

It is doubtful whether it is safe to rely upon the
voluntary action of the banks to revive the original
and essential complement of the clearing house loan
certificate, — the equalization of reserves. Fortunately, the usefulness of loan certificates would be

in no way diminished if their issue were made by law conditional upon the adoption of this means of preventing their use leading directly to the suspension of cash payments. Provided a central bank is established, the adoption of this proposal will become unnecessary since the certificates themselves would then not be needed. In its absence no other single remedy is so indispensable.

A more formal obstacle to the use of the reserves of the banks in emergencies should in any event be removed. The present law, in directing banks to discontinue lending operations when their reserves are deficient, works no great inconvenience in normal times, since the loans which are not taken by one bank can be taken by others. In emergencies, however, when all banks should use their reserves and if necessary go below reserve requirements, the general discontinuance of loans would prove more disastrous than the suspension of cash payments. The Comptroller of the Currency might be given the power to authorize the suspension of this particular provision of the law. The same purpose might be accomplished by permitting the banks to go below reserve requirements upon the payment of a tax high enough to have a deterrent but not a prohibitive effect.[1]

This paper has reached a length which forbids at this time any discussion of certain other aspects of our banking problem, in particular the disposition which should be made of the money of the government, and the bank-note question. The necessity

[1] See the suggestion to this effect by Professor C. W. Mixter, in the Quarterly Journal of Economics, February, 1908.

for some power to extend credit in the form of bank-
notes as a remedy in times of panic has, in my
opinion, been greatly exaggerated and has come to
overshadow other and more vital remedies. In any
event, it may be added in conclusion, the remedies
which have been suggested in these pages would to
a very considerable extent strengthen our banking
system, leaving a less formidable task to be performed
with the assistance of currency devices or by means
of a central bank.

CHAPTER III

PROPOSALS FOR STRENGTHENING THE EXISTING BANKS (CONCLUDED)

I

THE INELASTICITY OF BOND-SECURED NOTES

CURRENT discussion of banking reforms in the United States shows a noteworthy advance over that which followed the crisis of 1893. Attention was then concentrated upon monetary questions the solution of which was urgently required, and the defects of our credit machinery, in the absence of comprehensive analysis of its working, were too exclusively attributed to the bond-secured bank-notes. As a consequence, the improvement to be derived from some other method of issue was generally exaggerated. It is now coming to be recognized that the organization of credit rather than currency arrangements is, as was recently observed by Senator Aldrich, the fundamental banking problem, both in legislation and in practice. Certainly in those countries in which checks have become a well-nigh universal medium of payment, bank-notes, tho still a convenient instrument of credit, exercise an insignificant influence upon its organization. Experience with our own bond-secured notes affords ample and instructive confirmation of this view. It would be difficult to find any specific instance since the establishment of the national banking system when the notes have exerted an appreciable influence upon the credit structure or more than a very moderate influence upon the volume of credit granted to borrowers. Banking operations would have taken virtually the same course throughout the period even if the banks had possessed no right of issue and had only been able to extend credit in the form of deposit accounts. Some other method of issue may indeed increase somewhat the power of the banks to meet severe financial strain, but it will not remove any positive element of weakness now inherent in their organization or methods of business.

To most readers this view — of the harmlessness of the bond-secured notes — will seem to require very definite and convincing proof. For this reason it will be needful to analyze the effects of changes in the volume of circulation of the national banks since the establishment of the system. This analysis will at the same time prove to be a useful and even indispensable introduction to the discussion of the particular legislative proposals for a change in our method of issue which are to be brought forward.

Each of the short periods of severe strain through which the banks have passed since the establishment of the national system has been preceded by two much longer periods, one of depression and one of business activity and general economic advance. During these long periods every possible variety of movement in the issues of bank-notes has been witnessed. Before the crisis of 1873 the circulation had been practically stationary for some four years,

and indeed that was the situation regarding the
total supply of money in actual use.[1] During the
ten years to 1884 there were no pronounced fluctuations, tho the tendency was slightly downward.
From 1884 to 1891 circulation was rapidly retired;
then came a slow upward movement which continued
until 1900, followed by a far more considerable increase which has continued to the present time.
Alike in periods of depression and of business activity the circulation has increased, decreased, and
been stationary.

This failure of the notes to expand and contract
in response to changes in business requirements has
been often enough pointed out, but it has not been
observed that the changes which have occurred in
the volume of the notes have had practically no effect upon the condition of the banks. Throughout
the entire period of some forty years and quite without reference to changes in the circulation, the banks
have alternated between two well-defined situations.
During years of business depression their money
holdings have been well above reserve requirements
everywhere except in New York. On the other
hand, every period of business activity has witnessed
the rapid expansion of loans and consequently of
deposits until the reserve ratio was brought down
very close to the minimum required by law. There-
after, throughout the remainder of each period of
good times, loans and deposits have followed very

---

[1] The Act of July 12, 1870, provided for an addition of fifty-four million dollars to
the total circulation, but this increase was almost exactly offset by the coincident
retirement of the three per cent certificates which were largely held by the banks, being
available for reserve purposes.

closely changes in the available supply of money in
the banks. The last complete trade cycle may with
advantage be taken for illustration. Aside from
seasonal variations (which are of no importance for
the present purpose) the New York banks at all times
between 1894 and 1907 were working very close to
the twenty-five per cent requirement of the law and
the clearing house rule. The banks elsewhere were
well above reserve requirements during the first four
years of the period; then came a rapid decline in
the reserve ratio notwithstanding a large increase
in cash holdings. After 1901 there was no marked
change in the ratio of reserve to deposits; tho it may
be noted in passing that in 1902 and in 1906 it was
less than in 1907, just before the crisis. During this,
as well as in former periods (and, it may be added,
at the present time), there has been no reserve of
lending power anywhere among our banks except
in years of depression, when there was the least likelihood of its being needed.

II

Interest on Bankers' Deposits and Inelasticity

This unsatisfactory situation has been widely recognized and has been generally attributed to the
inevitable inelasticity of the bond-secured bank-notes.
A careful consideration of the forces at work, however, will show that its causes lie far deeper than currency arrangements, and that they are of a nature
which renders their removal a matter of the utmost
difficulty.

When business is generally inactive a relatively large part of the total money supply is held by the banks, on account of reduced requirements for cash for wages and other payments commonly made in those forms of the purchasing medium which pass readily from hand to hand. For this reason and because of the restricted demand of borrowers for loans, the banks in general have ample funds in excess of reserve requirements. In New York, however, as in the money centers of other countries, the demand for loans is at all times of practically indefinite proportions. Through the purchase of paper from note brokers and by means of stock exchange loans the New York banks can at all times fully employ their resources if they are willing to make sufficient concessions in rates to borrowers. This they are under the urgent necessity of doing as a consequence of the practice of paying interest on bankers' deposits at the fixed rate of two per cent, regardless of conditions in the loan market. To the effect of this practice is to be attributed the small surplus reserve held by the New York banks in years when the banks elsewhere find it impossible to employ all the funds which they are prepared to lend. But this practice of paying interest on bankers' deposits, as it now obtains, has other and more far-reaching consequences. It is an important cause of the failure to maintain a reserve of lending power in periods of business activity and the fundamental cause of the failure of the currency to contract in periods of depression. The bond requirement is in comparison an influence of slight moment. It is commonly believed that the banks make every effort to keep out their notes simply because they have been obliged to lock up slightly more than their equivalent in government bonds yielding a low rate of return. This is indeed one influence at work, but by no means the only one. Even tho this obstacle were removed through the substitution of some form of asset currency, interest on bankers' deposits would still prove an inducement sufficiently strong to prevent contraction. And further: it is this practice which makes it possible to keep out the bond-secured notes in periods of depression. Were it discontinued the banks would be utterly unable to prevent contraction, however strong their disinclination might be.

During periods of inactive trade the amount of bank-notes sent to Washington for redemption invariably reaches large proportions.[1] The city banks are chiefly responsible for this movement. Something like half the notes are sent in by the New York banks alone, which, when rates for call loans are persistently below two per cent, are naturally desirous of reducing bankers' balances swollen by the receipt of idle funds from all quarters. But the redemption of the notes does not secure contraction. All the banks,— more particularly the country banks and those of the smaller cities, — make haste to re-issue notes, thus setting free an equivalent amount of money, which in the absence of local demand is shipped to the money centers for the sake of the interest to be had from the city banks. There is a sort of endless chain, the work-

[1] During the year ending with October, 1907, national bank-notes to the amount of only $257,000,000 were sent to Washington for redemption. In 1908 the total reached $382,000,000 and for the year ending with October, 1909, it was $489,000,000.

ing of which can only be interrupted by the discontinuance (or some such modification as is suggested later) of the present practice of paying interest on bankers' deposits. Were that inducement removed, our bond-secured notes would prove to be susceptible to a considerable measure of contraction. Even if the banks continued to re-issue their notes as regularly as at present, contraction would still take place. An equivalent amount of money would be locked up in the banks, since they would reap no advantage from sending it to the money centers. Moreover, even if it were sent thither the pressure on city banks to force a demand for loans by the offer of low rates would be removed and they would doubtless maintain a higher reserve level.

This consequence of the payment of interest on deposits is quite independent of any particular conditions upon which the right of issue may be made to depend. If, for example, notes could have been issued during the last three years without any bond requirement, there is every reason to believe that something like the present volume of notes would be in circulation. The same possibility of keeping the notes out would have been present, and the inducement, tho slightly less urgent, would have been quite sufficient for the purpose. Finally, it may be noted that even if the banks had possessed no right of issue whatever, the situation would not have been essentially different. The aggregate supply of money in the country would then have been somewhat smaller, tho not by the full amount of the notes, since there would have been a somewhat greater amount of gold

within the country. Only such slight accumulation
of funds as may be due to this difference in the total
money supply can be properly attributed to the system of note issue.

This failure of the currency to contract during
periods of inactive business is after all a comparatively unimportant matter. At such times serious
difficulties are not likely to appear under any banking system, however imperfect. A certain amount
of unnecessary and unhealthy speculative activity
on the stock exchange is indeed made possible, but
its results, tho unfortunate to many individuals, are
not serious enough to deserve much public concern.

Turning now to periods of trade activity, we shall
find that here also none of the serious imperfections
in our banking system are to be attributed to the bond-
secured notes. At the outset loans everywhere are
increased, except in New York, where there is at no
time any considerable margin of idle credit. Indeed, the loan account of the New York banks is
rather more likely to be reduced than to increase.
Outside banks withdraw money to meet local requirements, and as rates advance purchase paper
more liberally from note brokers. A considerable
number of banks also, especially those of the other
cities, lend in the New York call loan market as soon
as rates rise well above the two per cent return on
balances.[1] Unless checked by premature trade reaction the general expansion of loans has always
continued until the banks reached the limits set by

[1] Between January, 1908, and August, 1909, the loans of the New York banks increased from $1,126,000,000 to $1,333,000,000, but during the following eight months
to May, 1910, they were reduced to $1,183,000,000.

the reserve requirements of the law. When periods of business activity happened to coincide with those in which the total money supply of the country was increasing, the upward movement of loans was particularly prolonged and considerable, since the banks always acquired some share in the increased stock of money. The taking out of additional circulation has therefore at times contributed to the enlargement of the foundation for credit expansion, but, owing to the limited supply of government bonds, prices have always responded to any widespread demand on the part of the banks, thus automatically checking any very considerable expansion in the issues of the notes. Moreover, even tho the expansion of loans has in some measure been made possible through the increase of the notes, it has not been in the slightest degree a result of any peculiar quality possessed by the notes on account of the bond requirement. Notes issued under quite different conditions would have had precisely the same effects if issued in equal quantity, and there is every reason to suppose that they would have been issued in even greater quantity. If, for example, the banks had been allowed to issue an asset currency, and the limit on the total issue had been above the amount of bond-secured notes actually put out by the banks, it is demonstrably certain that the volume of notes and consequently the amount of credit granted to borrowers would have been greater during each of our successive periods of business activity.

No system of redemption, however regular, can check the expansion of credit either in the form of

notes or of deposits when the loans of the banks are
being generally increased. The demand for loans
and the willingness of the banks to lend are the sole
determining factors so long as public confidence remains undisturbed. The redemption of such credit
instruments as checks and drafts is certainly speedy
and continuous, but it does not serve to prevent
the expansion of credit in the form of deposits
when all the banks are increasing their loans. It
does restrict the expanding of credit by a single
bank or by the banks of a single locality, at least
when borrowers use the proceeds of loans to make
purchases at a distance; but when all the banks of
the country are in question regular redemption
simply means larger exchanges of credit instruments
between the banks, either directly or through clearing houses. Exactly the same results will follow
the regular redemption of bank-notes, with the further qualification that the additional money always
required when employment is regular and wages are
high could be provided by the banks by means of
notes. The banks would then be shielded from one
cause of reserve loss, and would thus be able to increase loans still further before reaching the legal
minimum.

If the banks had had the power to issue as an asset
currency an amount of notes greater than that of
the bond-secured notes which have been actually in
circulation, it is certain that this right would have
been exercised long before the close of each of the
successive periods of business activity during the
last forty years. The loans of the banks have al-

ways kept pace with increases in money holdings,
even when these were being rapidly enlarged. Thus
between 1897 and 1907 the cash holdings of the
banks increased from $388,000,000 to $701,000,000, but
the expansion of loans and consequently of deposits
was even more considerable, so that the reserve ratio
at the end of the period was far less than at its beginning. That additional loans would have been
willingly absorbed by borrowers is also clear. In
this country of enterprising population and vast
undeveloped resources the demand for loans is of
practically indefinite proportions, except during years
of extreme depression. On the other hand, it would
hardly be maintained that the healthy progress of this
country has at any time suffered from inadequate credit
expansion; not infrequently the reverse has been true.

It is extremely doubtful also whether under any
feasible plan of asset currency there would be any
considerable quantity of notes available for emergency purposes. Some limit on the amount which
might be issued by the individual banks would be
a necessary feature of the safeguards designed to
protect note holders from loss. Assuming that this
limit would not be dangerously high, it is possible
and even probable that in the course of a long period
of almost uninterrupted prosperity, such as that
between 1897 and 1907, most of the banks would
have issued their entire quota. A few banks managed
with unusual foresight might perhaps retain their
notes for emergencies, but at the best the asset currency would be likely to prove a resource of very
limited value in time of crisis.

For somewhat analogous reasons no change in the method of issue can be relied upon to enable the banks to meet seasonal requirements for currency, such as those for crop-moving purposes. During the period (which might extend over a number of years) taken to expand the circulation to the limits fixed by law, no difficulties would be experienced. The situation would resemble that during years of inactive business in the past. Crop moving needs have at such times been met without difficulty, because the banks had ample funds in excess of reserve requirements. But after the banks had put out all their notes there would be a renewal of the difficulties with which we have been made familiar in the past. Temporarily idle funds would be attracted to the money centers by the interest to be secured for bankers' deposits. The winter and summer months would witness a plethora of money in New York while moderate withdrawals in the early spring and more considerable withdrawals in the autumn would again become a characteristic disturbing factor in our banking operations. The necessity of fully employing the funds secured through interest on deposits would continue to prevent the maintenance anywhere in our system of any reserve of lending power. This fundamental cause of weakness would be practically certain to wreck hopes of improvement from changes in our system of issue alone.

Why then, it may be asked, make any change, if the bond-secured notes have done so little positive harm, if slight improvement is to be gained and positive danger may be incurred by a change of system? The answer is two-fold. In the first place, even tho the bond-secured notes have never been issued in such quantities as to cause serious trouble, there is at least a possibility that they may have that effect in the future. If the government should be obliged to put out a large issue of bonds, the basis for a further and possibly excessive issue of notes would be provided. In the second place, it is undesirable that the bond policy of the government should be hampered by considerations of the effect of the purchase or sale of its securities upon the circulating medium. With the note issue entirely disassociated from the bonds the independent Treasury might easily be made a far less disturbing factor in the money market than it has often unavoidably been in the past. When, as at present, the Treasury has merely a working balance, it is a comparatively harmless institution. It is only when there has been a large surplus that its influence has been baneful. Between 1901 and 1907 the government surplus would doubtless have been expended in the purchase of bonds, if that could have been done without depriving the banks of the basis of their circulation. The unhealthy intervention of the Secretary of the Treasury in the money market would have been happily unnecessary.

The simplest way to remove the danger of an over-issue of the bond-secured notes and also to minimize the defects of the independent Treasury system would be to deprive the banks of the right of issue altogether. But there are economic reasons of weight against so drastic a remedy, and practical difficulties

of a political nature would seem to be insurmountable.
It would be necessary, in common fairness to the
banks, to increase the rate of interest on the two
per cent government bonds by at least one per cent,
so that they might be disposed of to investors without loss. Further, if the notes were retired, their
place would be taken by nearly an equivalent amount
of gold; thereby only could the level of prices in this
country be maintained in that relation to prices
elsewhere which our international trade conditions
have established. A costly medium of payment
(gold) would have to be substituted for an inexpen-
sive medium (bank-notes). If the gold foundation
of our monetary fabric were inadequate there would
be good reason for such a change; but the amount
of gold in the country is now ample for every purpose,
and is certain to be enlarged as a result of increasing
gold production, unless a great increase is made in
some of the other kinds of money now in circulation.
For these reasons it would seem inexpedient to deprive the banks of the right of issue, unless it should
prove impossible to devise currency arrangements
free from dangers of their own and without the defects
inherent in the bond-secured notes.

III

An Asset Currency of Limited Volume

With such distinctly moderate objects in view,
the following proposals for an asset currency are
submitted. It must be repeated, however, that
no material strengthening of our banking system is

to be expected while the present practice of paying interest on bankers' deposits continues.

Certain provisions necessary to protect note holders from loss have been made so familiar in previous discussions of an asset currency that they require no detailed consideration. The necessity that the notes should be made a prior lien on assets is everywhere recognized. In addition, a guarantee fund of five per cent is essential, not so much to protect note holders from ultimate loss as to prevent the discount on the notes of failed banks which would appear if payment were deferred until assets could be liquidated. But both the prior lien and the guarantee fund would have most undesirable consequences if no limits were placed upon the amount of notes which the individual banks might issue. It would be unfair to the depositor that his bank should be permitted to extend an indefinite amount of credit in a form which would have a preference in the distribution of assets. Moreover, if the note issue were equal to a considerable portion of the total assets, failures might subject the guarantee fund to heavy losses, the burden of which would fall upon the other banks.

It has commonly been proposed, therefore, that an asset currency should be limited to the capital of the banks. But this limit would permit at once the very large increase of nearly three hundred million dollars over the amount of notes now in circulation. Moreover, in the case of some banks, especially those of small size and those of recent origin, it would permit an issue dangerously large in proportion to total assets. For reasons already mentioned it does not seem desirable to grant the banks as a whole a power of issue which would make possible any immediate increase in the volume of notes. If the right of issue were limited to seventy per cent of the capital of the banks it would permit an issue almost exactly the same as that which we have at present. A far better basis for limitation of issue, however, is the capital and surplus of the banks. Measured in this way, the ratio would be not seventy per cent on capital, but forty per cent on capital and surplus. It would be far better to take capital and surplus rather than capital alone, because surplus usually increases with the life and growth of business of the banks. The assets of such banks are likely to be large with reference to the liability of share holders. Forty per cent of capital and surplus, therefore, is likely to be a smaller portion of the total assets of the banks than seventy per cent of capital, and consequently there is less likelihood that in case of failure the resources of a bank would prove insufficient to meet the notes. As a further precaution no bank should be granted the right of issue until after it had been in business for some two or three years, long enough to test the character of its management.

Finally, since the notes would be a form of credit pure and simple, they should be protected by the same ratio of reserve that is required against deposits, thus restoring a provision of the National Banking Law which was repealed, by inadvertence rather than by intent, in 1874.[1] This requirement would tie up a certain amount of money in reserves, but as the banks would probably convert some part of their undivided profits into surplus in order to be able to take out additional circulation, no contraction in the money in actual use would be likely to result.

There remains for consideration one further provision necessary to complete this proposal for a change in our method of note issue. The bond-secured notes are taxed either one or one-half of one per cent, according to the issues of bonds which have been deposited as security by the banks. Notes issued under the conditions which have just been outlined could easily bear the heavier burden of a two per cent tax. By this simple means revenue more than sufficient to place the two per cent government bonds on an investment basis would be provided without increasing the burdens of general taxation.

Notes issued under these conditions would provide an absolutely safe circulating medium. Note holders could not by any possibility suffer loss, and while there would be room for slow growth along with that of the capital and surplus of the banks, the danger of over-issue would be wholly eliminated. If it should be found that these notes were kept out as persistently as the bond-secured notes, no new element of

[1] The Act of June 20, 1874, as passed was a fragment of a far more comprehensive measure relating both to banking and the greenbacks. The banks were to be required to hold all of their reserves in vault, but as a partial offset, the five per cent redemption fund authorized by the act was made available for reserve purposes, and no reserve was required against circulation. In conference the last two provisions were retained, altho the requirement with which they had been associated, while the bill was being passed through the two Houses, — namely, that the banks should hold all their reserves, — was deleted in deference to hostility to contraction. For further details, see the writer's History of Crises under the National Banking System, pp. 105-107.

weakness would be introduced, and some of the disadvantages of the present system would be removed. It would be no small gain to have severed the entangling alliance between government bonds and currency. Moreover, it should be observed that the proposed issue is of a nature to permit without difficulty such further modifications as experience with its working may suggest. It is indeed unlikely that the policy of holding notes in reserve to meet seasonal or emergency requirements would be adopted by a sufficient number of the banks to make the notes an elastic medium. If, however, this should prove happily a mistaken prediction, the amount of notes which each bank might issue could be made greater without difficulty, and to the general advantage.

It would be a simple matter also to grant the banks the power to issue an additional heavily taxed circulation upon terms which would make certain that it would be exercised only in emergencies. From what has been said on previous pages, it would seem to follow that so long as the present practice of paying interest on bankers' deposits continues, a currency to meet extraordinary occasions can only be secured in this way. But against an emergency circulation of any kind lies the serious objection that it would weaken still further the already inadequate influences tending to restrain excessive credit expansion in periods of active business. It is to be feared that bankers would rely too exclusively upon the taxed notes, and that, altho they might do something to ameliorate financial disturbances, they would increase rather than diminish the likelihood of their occurrence.

IV

CHANGE IN METHOD OF PAYING INTEREST ON BANKERS' DEPOSITS

An asset currency such as has been outlined above would without doubt have the desired quality of elasticity, if the payment of interest on bankers' deposits were entirely discontinued. Thirty or more years ago there was a very widespread sentiment among bankers against the practice, but any proposal for its discontinuance would now meet with violent and general opposition, and its adoption could only be secured through legal enactment. Moreover, however effective for the purpose, so drastic a remedy would have other consequences which make its adoption not only inexpedient, but also upon the whole undesirable.

If banking in this country were conducted by a few hundred banks, each having numerous branches, loanable funds would be readily transferred from place to place in response to variations in the requirements of borrowers. No payments for bankers' deposits would be needed for the purpose, and they would be contrary to the interests of the several banks. But with our numerous independent local banks, that inducement is requisite to secure even the imperfect utilization of such funds of the several banks as may be in excess of local requirements. Tho motives of business convenience would in any case lead the banks to keep some balances with the banks of the money centers, their amount would be insignificant in comparison with that which has been secured through the offer of interest. These balances are undesirably large, as was pointed out in the first part of Chapter II; but they should be reduced by measures which would enable the banks to employ safely additional funds at home at more profitable rates than the two per cent received from the city banks. The extreme remedy of a complete prohibition of interest on bankers' deposits would be a hardship to all classes of banks, and would involve the wasteful locking up of funds in the vaults of each of the many thousands of banks in the country outside the money centers. Doubtless the individual banks would lend directly a larger portion of their funds than at present, but in so doing, they would probably be tempted into making undesirable loans at home, and greater investments in the loan markets of New York and of the other large cities.

The utilization of the entire resources of the banks is not consistent with absolute safety under any system, because of the need of some reserve of lending power to meet emergencies. But only as a last resort should a measure be adopted which would prove an insurmountable obstacle to the employment by some banks of the more or less permanent surplus funds of other banks through deposits with city agents. Fortunately the ill effects of the present method of paying interest on such deposits can be diminished, if not entirely removed, without entailing any undesirable curtailment of the employment of banking resources. It is not necessary in order to make conditions favorable to an elastic currency that the city banks should hold no bankers' balances, or only those required in connection with the domestic exchanges. It is only necessary to prevent the movement to and from the money centers of the temporarily idle funds of the country banks, those which will be certainly needed by them after a very short interval. The present method of paying interest on bankers' deposits gives the city banks a highly irregular lending power which is of advantage neither to them nor to the community, because there are no variations in business requirements which coincide with the seasonal variations in the amount of funds at the disposal of the city banks. If there were an end to temporary accessions of funds from the country in the winter and early summer months, the average as well as the maximum loan account of the city banks would indeed be somewhat reduced, but it is probable that profits would not be diminished to any appreciable extent. It is even possible that they would be increased, since rates for loans, especially the call loan rate, would be maintained at a higher level, and the interest to be paid outside banks would be reduced.

A very simple modification of the present practice of paying interest on bankers' deposits would do much to check this unhealthy seasonal movement of money in and out of the money centers. It is only necessary that instead of daily balances, the minimum balance kept in the course of a considerable period be taken as the basis for reckoning the interest to be paid to depositing banks. This period should be one of sufficient length to cover an entire movement of money in and out of the banks. Six months would seem to be the most natural and effective term for the accomplishment of the purpose in view. This method of reckoning interest would clearly be of advantage to the city banks, and would tend to greater stability in dealings upon the stock exchange. It would also give elasticity to the currency, because the country banks could then gain no advantage from keeping out all of their notes at all times. That practice would only succeed in building up balances with city banks which could not be maintained for the entire six months' period. The return received by the country banks would indeed be somewhat diminished, but not beyond what was expedient for them and for the community. There would, however, be reasonable ground for complaint in particular cases if the interest return were to be reckoned upon the basis of the minimum balance during a six months period. The course of payments may momentarily bring down the balance of a country bank with a city agent to an abnormally low point, and a considerable reduction of the interest return owing to such a chance occurrence would be obviously inequitable. To meet this situation, the basis of interest should be the minimum weekly, fortnightly, or even monthly balance during the period of six months.

On account of the very slight change proposed in present practice regarding interest on bankers' deposits, its fundamental importance is perhaps in danger of being overlooked. To the writer it promises more far-reaching results than any of the other proposals with which this paper and that which preceded have been concerned. Only in case some such change is made does it seem possible to secure an elastic currency by the substitution of an asset note issue for our bond-secured notes. By its means some reserve of lending power will be insured, and at the same time the character of banking operations in ordinary times will be influenced for the better. Remove the accumulation of temporarily idle funds from the city banks, and the call loan may perchance lose some of that false glamor of liquidness which has been perhaps the greatest bane to sound banking in this country. Within narrow limits it is of course true that no other kind of loan can be liquidated so quickly. For this reason it has been especially well suited to the employment of funds only momentarily in the possession of the banks. But the easy facility with which such loans can be slightly increased or diminished has probably contributed more than anything else to foster a trust in the indefinite liquidness of call loans which every emergency in our history has shown to be absolutely without foundation.

V

SUMMARY

Let me now summarize the series of proposals which have been brought forward in this and the preceding paper. The establishment of true savings departments by the national banks, with segregated deposits payable at notice, which might be invested in mortgages, was advocated as a means of enabling the banks to employ a greater part of their funds at home. Some diminution in the amount of the balances in the banks of the money centers would follow, thus reducing the strain upon them in emergencies. Further, as the present reserve against deposits could be safely reduced upon those demand deposits which would be converted into time deposits, the money thus set free would enable the banks to increase the ratio of reserve against their remaining demand deposits. A cash reserve of ten per cent was accordingly suggested for country banks. As a further means of strengthening reserves, a plan for two classes of banks, local banks and reserve agent banks, was outlined to take the place of the present three classes. Both classes of banks might be established anywhere, but those choosing to become reserve agent banks would be required to have a minimum capital of five hundred thousand dollars, and would be obliged to carry a cash reserve of twenty-five per cent. Provisions to render more certain the use of reserves in emergencies were then outlined. The banks should be allowed to go below reserve requirements upon the payment of a fine, sufficiently onerous to insure the maintenance of reserves in normal times, but not so high as to prevent their use when really needed. In addition, it was urged as absolutely necessary that reserves should be pooled or equalized, whenever clearing house loan certificates are issued, in order to prevent that working at cross purposes among the banks, which has been the principal cause of suspension of cash payments in the past.

The proposal for an asset currency made in the present paper is so framed as to insure safety, and a very moderate increase in the total circulation in the future. In itself it is not expected to strengthen our banking system materially; but by securing the separation of the circulating medium from the government bonds, it would enable the government to avoid the accumulation of a large surplus in the Treasury in the future. The change in note issue, however, if accompanied with the proposed modification of the present practice of paying interest on bankers' deposits by the city banks would give a considerable degree of elasticity to the currency.

At the outset the opinion was expressed that a central bank of the European type was at best a doubtful remedy for our financial ills, and that less revolutionary means gave more certain promise of improvement. But even to those who are convinced that only by means of a central organization of some kind can the fundamental defects in our system be removed, these proposals should not be unwelcome.[1] Their adoption would create no obstructions to the establishment of a central bank, and most of them would clearly tend to increase the likelihood of successful results from its operation. The establishment of savings departments by the national banks, in so far as it would strengthen our system as a whole, would lessen the calls upon the central bank for assistance in emergencies. Similarly, the proposals designed to strengthen the reserves of the banks, and to render

---

[1] It is significant that the proposals of some of the most earnest opponents of a central bank of the European type, such as Congressman C. N. Fowler and Mr. Victor Morawetz, include provision for the centralized control of our banking system.

them more willing to make use of them, could not
fail to lighten the burden upon the central institution.
Some of the plans for a central bank do indeed provide
for the concentration of the entire banking reserve
of the country, but so complete a reversal of existing
practice would seem to be altogether unlikely to
secure general favor. The requirement that reserves be equalized when clearing house loan certificates are issued would probably be found unnecessary if a central bank were established. It is essential to the successful working of a central bank
that clearing house balances, at least in the important cities, be settled through transfers on its books.
Clearing house loan certificates, therefore, would become unnecessary, and consequently also the equalization of reserves. The proposal regarding note
issue would not be inimical to a central bank plan,
but rather the reverse. It would not be an obstacle
to the grant to the central bank of a special privilege
of issue, a right that might well prove more advantageous than a complete monopoly of this power.
The bank would be relieved of the burden of taking
care of the bonds now held by the banks against
circulation. Moreover, it would make it far more
easy for its management to resist the pressure for
accommodation when for any reason the further
expansion of credit should be deemed inadvisable.
Finally, the proposal regarding interest on bankers'
deposits loses nothing of its importance. Indeed,
its importance is perhaps enhanced. The most
difficult problem which confronts central banks,
and the one which they have to face most frequently,

is the control or restraint of the central money markets in the various countries in which they have been established. To exert any effective restraining power over the credit situation in New York would certainly be more frequently necessary, and more difficult to accomplish, if the other banks continued to receive large temporary accessions of funds from outside banks.

In the first paper in this series (originally published in May, 1909), I set forth at length the peculiar difficulties with which a central bank would be confronted in this country. Primarily on account of the absence of branch banking, it was contended that methods which had proved effective in European countries were not certain to have similar results with us. It has now become more generally recognized that if our banking system is to be strengthened by means of a central bank, the character of its operations, far more than the form of organization, must be carefully worked out, and that while European central banks may furnish valuable suggestive material, they cannot serve as models to be more or less exactly reproduced. On the other hand, the proposal to establish a central bank, or at least some kind of centralized authority, has been received with far greater favor than most persons familiar with our financial history would have anticipated. Some of the objections raised in my earlier article have been met in the subsequent discussion of the subject, but the various plans which have been brought forward are not free from those of most serious import. There is also a common tendency to rely wholly upon a central bank to remove the defects in our banking system. But since the effects of the operations of such a bank in this country are more or less uncertain, it would seem to be the part of wisdom as a preliminary measure to strengthen our system by the adoption of such other changes as are not incompatible with the operations of a central bank. The burden placed upon it at the outset should be made light, and its activities should be allowed to develop themselves along lines which experience with its working may suggest. With these modest purposes in view, it is my intention in a concluding paper to return to the consideration of the central bank problem. I shall attempt to suggest a plan for a central bank or central organization with limited functions and responsibilities, which will meet the difficulties which have impressed me perhaps more strongly than other writers upon this important subject.

CHAPTER IV

A CENTRAL BANK OF LIMITED SCOPE

I

THE present paper will be concerned entirely with the elucidation of a plan for a central bank; but as the effectiveness of the plan would largely depend upon the adoption of the proposals which were brought forward in the two preceding articles in this series, these proposals may be summarized here by way of introduction. The establishment of true savings departments by the national banks with segregated deposits payable at notice, which might be invested in mortgages, was advocated as a means of enabling the banks to employ more of their funds at home, thus reducing somewhat the strain upon the city banks in emergencies. Two classes of banks, local and reserve agent banks, were proposed to take the place of the present three classes. Both classes of banks might be established anywhere, but those choosing to become reserve agent banks would be required to have a minimum capital of $500,000 and would be obliged to carry a cash reserve of 25 per cent, a cash reserve of 10 per cent being required from local banks. In order to render more certain the use of reserves in emergencies it was suggested that the banks should be allowed to go below reserve requirements upon the payment of a fine sufficiently onerous to insure the maintenance of reserves in normal times, but not so high as to prevent their use when really needed. An asset currency limited in amount to 40 per cent of the capital and surplus of the banks was proposed, to take the place of the bond-secured notes. This separation of the circulating medium from government bonds would enable the government to avoid the accumulation of a large surplus in the Treasury in the future, and a tax of 2 per cent on the notes would provide the means for placing the bonds held by the banks upon an investment basis. Finally, it was pointed out that elasticity can not be secured while the present practice of paying interest on bankers' deposits continues. The payment of interest upon minimum weekly or fortnightly balances during a period of six months was suggested as a way out of this unsatisfactory condition of affairs.

The adoption of these proposals would diminish materially in emergencies the strain upon the reserve-holding banks of the cities and would also increase somewhat and make more available the money holdings of the banks generally. But while the power to meet the demand for loans and also that for cash from depositors would be increased, it must be admitted that no absolute certainty is secured against that senseless scramble between the banks to strengthen themselves which more than anything else has caused the breakdown of our credit machinery on every occasion of severe strain in the past. Bankers must have confidence in the means at their disposal, and the public must have unquestioned trust not only in the ultimate solvency of the banks but also in the

ability of the banks to maintain payments at all
times; otherwise, no system, however strong it may
be, can endure the strain incidental to trade reaction
without danger of financial panic.

Now, altho one may feel convinced that the means
which have been suggested would be ample to enable
the banks to handle emergencies effectively, it becomes
evident that something more is needed when we find
that the officers of our large reserve-holding city
banks are of the opinion that, even with a very considerable increase in the ratio of their cash holdings
to deposit liabilities, it would be impossible to respond
to the demands which would be made upon them by
country banks in a crisis of the severity of that of
1907. On the other hand, there is apparently a
widespread and growing belief among bankers that
difficulties which have proved overwhelming in the
past can be met and even removed through the establishment of some kind of central bank or central
authority in our banking system. It is urged, and
with much reason, that the results achieved in all
countries which have made trial of institutions of
this kind would give it an initial prestige which would
be a source of great strength. It is also pointed out
that we should then have a banking influence exercised
with a deep sense of responsibility, and above all that
we should have a reserve of cash and of lending power
which could certainly be turned to in emergencies.

The promise of improvement through the establishment of a central bank would seem to be bright
if it is so devised as to fit into our existing complex
banking machinery. This possibility does not, how-

ever, lessen the importance of proposals designed to strengthen the existing banks such as those with which the preceding articles have been concerned. On the contrary their importance is rather enhanced if the attainment of the desired results is to be secured through the device of a central bank. The danger that other banks will rely wholly upon it for assistance in emergencies is one which must be squarely faced. The restraining power which a central institution can exercise in periods of business activity over twenty thousand or more independent local banks is certainly slight, far less than that over the comparatively small number of banks in European countries in which branch banking prevails. Influenced by competition and the natural desire for large profits, our banks as a whole have shown no evidence of any appreciable willingness to maintain themselves in a stronger condition than was required by law. It is to be feared that the mere existence of a central bank will tend to foster the growth of unsound conditions by relieving the other banks of all sense of responsibility. Moreover, should the entire burden in emergencies be imposed upon the central bank, its power to make loans and to extend credit must be of colossal magnitude if it is to be able to prevent the complete breakdown of our credit machinery. On the other hand, regarded simply as one feature of a plan for strengthening our banking system, a central bank with restricted functions and power can be devised which gives far more certain promise of improvement.

In the first article of this series originally published in May, 1909, I pointed out at some length that the

most serious and, perhaps, insurmountable obstacle
to the successful working of a central bank in this
country is found in the employment in normal times
of even a part of the vast lending power which was
an essential feature of all the plans for such an institution which had been brought forward. Nor has
this difficulty been overcome in any of the proposals
which have subsequently appeared. Further reflection, however, has led me to the conclusion that a
central bank is feasible for this country; but only
upon two conditions. In the first place, the adoption
of measures designed to strengthen the other banks
is necessary in order to diminish the strain upon the
central bank and consequently the need of granting
it the colossal lending power which will otherwise be
indispensable. In the second place, it must be generally recognized that it is not the primary function
of a central bank to strengthen our system by means
of the advances which it may make to other banks.
Through a central bank the machinery can be provided which will prevent the scramble between the
banks to strengthen themselves in emergencies and
which will also greatly diminish the withdrawals of
cash by individual depositors except from banks whose
solvency is in question. If this can be accomplished
it would never be necessary for a central bank to
make large advances to the other banks. Its lending
function would be distinctly secondary and its power
to extend credit could be limited to such comparatively small proportions that the difficulty of handling
its loan account in normal times would not be of
serious moment. But to most of those who are favor-

ably inclined towards the central bank proposal much of its attractiveness is found in the improvements in our credit arrangements which are expected from its lending operations. Moreover, the view that a central bank with extensive lending power can not be made to fit into our system has been controverted by high authority [1] and the conclusion that this view is without real foundation has gained wide acceptance. For these reasons it seems advisable to give some further consideration to the matter before introducing the particular proposal which is the main concern of this article.

Foreign example, tho helpful, must be followed with extreme caution on account of some fundamental peculiarities in our banking organization and practice. The power of banks to extend credit in the form of deposits is restricted in all countries having a central bank, with the single exception of England, on account of the limited use of checks. Consequently when a given amount of accommodation is secured from the central bank the other banks are not able to make very much more than an equivalent increase in their own loans. The effect of advances made by the Bank of England is far more considerable. Upon the notes of the Bank as till money and upon balances at the Bank as reserves rests the vast deposit credit structure of the other banks. Except when the proceeds of loans are being used to meet foreign obligations or payments to the government, advances by the Bank of England serve to increase, tho indirectly, the foundation upon which the other banks extend credit in

[1] See Paul M. Warburg's A United Reserve Bank of the United States, pp. 32–42.

the form of deposits to several times their amount.[1] The lending operations of the Bank do not, however, result in dangerous credit expansion because its power to extend loans is not great, and even that limited power is exercised with great caution. It is unable to extend credit in the form of notes, since its note is virtually a gold certificate; and tho its deposit credits have the same effect upon the lending power of the other banks, the general economic and financial position of the London money market seldom permits of their rapid increase. A large amount of foreign money is regularly employed there, and any considerable increase in the loans of the Bank would at once depress rates and induce the withdrawal of foreign lenders.

In the United States the expansive effect upon the volume of credit of the advances made by a central bank, whether in the form of notes or deposits, would be similar in kind to that noted in the case of the Bank of England. But the difficulties to be met would be far more unmanageable. It is agreed upon all hands that there is no likelihood of securing favorable action upon a plan for a central bank if it is to compete in any substantial way with existing banks. Its loans are to be made to the other banks either in the form of notes, which, unlike those of the Bank of England, are to be credit instruments; or in the form of deposits on its books. Both its notes and deposits would be considered (and necessarily so if the bank is to be able to handle emergencies) as reserves by the other banks.

[1] The process is indirect because the other banks do not rediscount at the Bank of England. It is the withdrawal of money lent to bill brokers, who in turn are obliged to borrow from the Bank, which serves to increase bankers' balances at the central institution.

Upon these reserves they would without much doubt gradually build up deposit credits to the extent permitted by law or, in the absence of legal limitation, to such limits as might be deemed safe by the officers of the individual banks.

It is contended, however, that the danger of excessive credit expansion resulting from the operations of a central bank would be slight because the Bank would rediscount only paper of the very highest quality, and that it would be overcome entirely by means of a sliding scale of discount. But the character of the security which will be acceptable will not appreciably affect the situation one way or the other. Practically all banks have some paper which would meet the most exacting of tests. The root of the difficulty is found in the use which will be made of the additional lending power thus secured by the other banks. While in some instances this power might be used to make further loans of the same high character, there is quite as great a possibility of its employment in underwriting syndicates or in collateral loans to customers the proceeds of which will be used for speculative purposes. Any single bill or note rediscounted would of course mature within a comparatively short time, but in so far as a steady amount of rediscounts were made by the central bank to a particular bank or in a particular locality, the basis for credit expansion to a much greater extent would be provided.

The effectiveness of a sliding rate of discount in preventing undue credit expansion is also far from certain. Where, as in England, foreign financial dealings are large relatively to those of purely domestic origin, the course of the foreign exchanges is a delicate barometer of the credit position, and it is a comparatively easy matter for the officers of central banks to adjust their rates to meet changing circumstances. In the United States the credit furnished by the banks is almost entirely utilized for domestic purposes. Excessive credit expansion is but remotely reflected in the market for foreign exchange. It would, therefore, be unusually difficult for the central bank to adjust its rates so as to promote business activity when that would be of general advantage and to exercise restraint when that becomes necessary.

But there is a far more serious obstacle to successful results from a sliding scale of discount. Partly on account of the differences in the average quality of loans but mainly on account of the absence of branch banking, there is a wide difference in lending rates between various sections of the country. If the central bank is to lend everywhere at a rate which would just make it of advantage for the banks of the eastern money centers to resort to it for discounts, it would be overwhelmed with requests for loans from banks in those sections of the country in which rates are high and an excessive proportion of its funds would be thus absorbed. It might, indeed, lend at different rates in the various sections. But it is extremely unlikely that public opinion would tolerate such differences, especially if the bank were granted a monopoly of issue and held large government deposits. The demand that lending resources be distributed evenly has not occasioned serious difficulty to central

banks in other countries,[1] but in the United States
there is certain to be such a demand, because owing
to the absence of branch banking it would be one of
an entirely reasonable nature.

Credit is but imperfectly fluid in a system of numerous independent local banks. Loanable funds flow
readily from country banks and those of small cities
to the large cities and especially to New York. But
with us, unlike the countries with branch banking,
the movement goes no further. Our money centers
are reservoirs for the collection of funds which can
not be employed either temporarily or permanently
at home, but they are unsatisfactory distributing
agents. There are, indeed, many instances of temporary advances by reserve agents to country banks
which are not inconsiderable in amount, but taking
the country banks as a whole they get even temporarily from the money centers comparatively little
beyond what they have deposited or employed there.
As for permanent requirements in excess of local
banking resources, they can hardly be said to be met
at all by the transfer of surplus funds from other
localities. In England it makes little difference
where or to whom the Bank of England makes its
advances. Credit may be likened to a reservoir the
general level of which is raised or lowered by the loans
of the central bank. In this country there are as
many reservoirs as there are banks or at least localities. Loans made by a central bank in Boston or
Baltimore or even in New York would not enable

---

[1] The agrarian demand for agricultural credits has been the nearest approach in
Continental countries.

banks in Seattle or Galveston to lend more freely.
In these circumstances a central bank would be obliged
to lend in each locality and enormous pressure would
be brought to bear to remove any obstacle, such as
a discriminating rate of discount, even tho it might
be based upon the soundest of banking principles.
And in carrying through contraction the management
of a central bank would be faced by an even more
perplexing problem. It would be necessary to consider the situation in each locality and to apply pressure only where credit had been expanded beyond
safe limits and in proportion to the extent of the
expansion. Can we expect local opinion to coincide
generally with that of the management of a central
bank ? Often, it is to be feared, aggrieved localities
would feel that they were being treated less liberally
in the case of expansion and more severely in the case
of contraction than neighboring and competing communities.

II

All these difficulties, it will be observed, have a
common origin. They will disappear if it can be
shown that a central bank can perform its essential
functions without that enormous lending power which
will bring upon it an irresistible demand for accommodation from other banks in periods of active business. It would then be recognized at the outset that
it is not to be primarily a lending institution and that
its powers can be so limited as to shield it from unreasonable requirements.

There is a consensus of opinion that the withdrawal and hoarding of cash in emergencies by both individuals and banks has been due not so much to doubt of ultimate solvency as to fear that the banks would temporarily suspend. If this fear can be removed, emergency requirements for cash and the consequent sudden contraction of loans to which the banks have resorted in the past, would no longer be of serious moment. The mere existence of a central bank firmly established in public confidence would largely do away with those temporarily large cash requirements which have proved too heavy a burden for banks. Certainly it would not have been necessary for it to pay out any such quantity of money as would have been needed by existing banks in order to allay distrust in any one of our past crises.

But the diminution in cash withdrawals through the establishment of a central bank is not limited to the general effect of the greater confidence in our banking system which it might create. Through its means more direct influences can be exerted which will so reduce emergency withdrawals that they will become a negligible factor in the working of our credit machinery. This can be accomplished with advantage to the other banks and without involving any loss of liberty in the management of their affairs. The means are very simple: it is only necessary to make the central bank the organ for settlements of clearing house balances in the important cities and also for handling payments and transfers of money between different sections of the country. In other words, its primary function would be that of a clearing house for the entire country with which the other banks would become so closely related in normal times that it would be entirely unlikely that the connection would be severed in emergencies.

The importance attached to this function is the fundamental novelty in the present central bank proposal. Its significance must therefore receive somewhat detailed exposition.

The ordinary clearing house affords a familiar indication of what may be accomplished through a central bank in economizing the use of money by diminishing the aggregate withdrawals from the banks and by making them more regular in amount from day to day. A clearing house has the immediately practical function of simplifying the daily settlements between the banks of a locality. But its operation has another and even more important result: that of reducing very largely the amount of money required in the conduct of banking, at least in normal times. If, for example, each bank in New York made daily cash settlements with all the other banks of the city singly, it is obvious that a very much larger part of the money holdings of the banks would be in constant use. It might even happen that all the money held by a bank would be paid out in meeting unfavorable balances with some of the banks, tho it might be more than replaced in the course of the day by money received from the remaining banks against which it had favorable balances. Clearly, then, if clearing balances were settled by means of transfers on the books of a central bank instead of with cash there would be a still further economy in its use.

This is the London practice; and it reduces materially the amount of coin or notes which would otherwise be withdrawn day by day from the Bank of England. The aggregate balances of the other banks at the Bank of England may remain stationary while wide fluctuations may be of daily occurrence in that of any particular bank. Fluctuating withdrawals of cash are avoided which, even tho temporary, would make it necessary for the Bank to hold a larger reserve than is now required.

Economizing the use of cash is not, however, the most important result which would follow from the settlement of clearing house balances through a central bank. It would stand ready to make advances when necessary to banks whose reserves had been depleted. The possibility of securing such accommodation would render entirely unnecessary the resort to the issue of clearing house loan certificates in emergencies. Advances by the central bank would be far more effective because they could be made without the delay and inevitable publicity which destroys much of the usefulness of that instrument as an emergency device. Moreover, the working at cross purposes among the banks, which in the absence of provision for the equalization of reserves has always continued after the issue of loan certificates, would be entirely prevented.[1] The central bank would be in position to refuse accomodation to banks seeking to strengthen

[1] This subject is discussed in Chapter II. It is much more fully treated in the writer's History of Crises under the National Banking System recently published by the National Monetary Commission. See especially references under Clearing House Loan Certificates and Equalization of Reserves in the index.

themselves unnecessarily when well able to meet their
obligations with their own cash resources.

It is to be assumed that the central bank, if it is to
perform such functions in any adequate fashion,
would establish branches in all the important commercial and financial cities of the country. Let it
be assumed also that settlement of clearing house
balances would generally be made by means of transfers on its books. Then the following results of the
first importance would follow. The Bank would be
enabled to handle much business by means of deposit
credits on its books which would otherwise involve
the issue of notes or the withdrawal of coin from its
reserves. The pressure on the Bank in emergencies
would be materially diminished, because it would
be in position to insist upon the use of the cash resources of the other banks. This would be a very
great gain, especially if means of strengthening the
other banks, such as were urged in the two preceding
articles, should be adopted. Instead of relieving the
other banks of their responsibilities, the central bank,
it will be seen, would exert a powerful influence in
securing the regular performance of their duties.
Finally, the vital cause of weakness which has invariably manifested itself on every occasion of crisis would
largely disappear. At such times our banking system
has been subjected to intolerable strain because of
the wholesale withdrawal by country banks and those
of the smaller cities of balances deposited in the banks
of the large cities and especially in the banks of New
York. Tho unreasoning fear has prompted this
action to some extent, the main cause has been the

well-grounded belief that the city banks would discontinue currency shipments and temporarily suspend payments. Confidence that payments will be maintained by city banks will certainly do much to reduce withdrawals within limits set by the actual needs of the country banks, and those needs will in turn be greatly lessened if individual depositors acquire confidence in the capacity of the banking system as a whole to meet occasions of severe strain.

There remains for consideration still another means for diminishing and regularizing the movements of cash between banks by means of facilities which can be provided by a central bank. At present many banks are separated by enormous distances from their reserve agents. When a bank thus situated finds it necessary to increase its cash holdings, either to meet regular requirements, such as those for crop-moving purposes, or in order to be on the safe side in emergencies, it will naturally call for a larger shipment of currency from city banks than there is any great likelihood that it will be obliged to use. The available statistics tho incomplete indicate that very much more money is withdrawn from city banks every autumn than is actually used by the country banks for crop-moving purposes.

This defect in our system can be remedied and at the same time other important advantages gained if the central bank establishes a system for handling the domestic exchanges between all the places in which it has branches, by means of which all payments between banks can be met by transfers on its books. The Reichsbank has perfected a system of this sort which has proved of great advantage, making it possible to make payments throughout the country speedily and at a minimum of expense.[1] The service is open both to banks and to individuals, the only condition being the maintenance of a balance at the Bank the amount of which is determined by the volume of transfers in each particular instance. Whether in case such a system is adopted in this country it should be available for individuals need not be definitely decided at the outset. Until the machinery is perfected it would seem the wiser course to restrict its use to the banks alone. The economy in the use of cash which might be secured in this way is evident. Suppose a bank in Utah were to draw upon its balance in some one of the New York banks. The latter would simply transfer the amount through the central bank to the branch of the central bank in the vicinity of the Utah correspondent. The latter, having its funds in its immediate neighborhood, would only draw them out gradually from day to day as the need arose. Moreover, the central bank would not have to ship funds from New York; even if, like the Bank of England, it were only able to issue a note which is merely a gold certificate, it would still be able to keep a supply of its notes at all of its branches, and from this supply it could pay out anywhere an amount of notes equal to its cash holdings, which would doubtless be largely concentrated in New York. Finally, it may be noted that this system would make it impossible for the reserve-holding city banks to refuse to meet the de-

[1] For full details regarding the Giro-verkehr system of the Reichsbank see the volume entitled Miscellaneous Articles on German Banking, pp. 171-213, published by the National Monetary Commission.

mands of their banking depositors for funds. The
country bank would be able to send a draft on its
reserve agent for collection through the central bank
and this draft would go through the clearing house
in the city where the reserve agent was situated.

Apart from its importance in emergencies a universal
system of transfers through a central bank would
have important advantages in normal times. The
present situation regarding the domestic exchanges
is far from satisfactory either to the business community or to the banks. Collections and payments
are subject to delay and involve heavy expense, burdensome to most banks tho to some extent shifted
upon their customers. Practically the entire expense
of the domestic exchanges could be saved. The actual
cost to the central bank would be far less than that
inevitable under the present system, or lack of system;
and such expenses as it would incur would be met by
the profits arising from the balances which the other
banks would be obliged to maintain in order to make
use of the service. The maintenance of these balances
need not be an added expense to the banks, even tho
no interest upon them could be allowed. Such balances might properly be included as a part of the
required cash reserves of the banks, not merely a
part of their reserves which may be deposited with
other banks. It seems neither necessary nor desirable
to overturn our present system of deposited reserves
by taking away a large portion of the funds with which
the present reserve-holding banks conduct their business and transferring them to a central bank. Such
a great change would make the central bank an insti-

tution of unwieldy size and would deprive country banks of all return upon that part of their reserve; and it might lead to a wasteful retention of all their required reserve in the form of cash in their own vaults. The plan proposed would give the central bank a moderate volume of bankers' deposits, leaving the present arrangement unchanged aside from the modifications suggested in the second article of this series.

One further means of improvement remains for consideration. It is closely related to the proposal which has just been discussed, but does not involve any action on the part of a central bank. In a country so large as the United States it would be difficult and perhaps undesirable to establish a system for collection of all checks through a single institution. Tho experience might indicate that such an arrangement was feasible, it would greatly simplify matters at the outset to provide through a central bank only the machinery needed to make transfers between the localities in which it might open branches, leaving to the various clearing houses the task of handling settlements in their immediate neighborhood. Already a few clearing houses (among which that of Boston is the most important) have in successful operation arrangements for handling checks from surrounding country banks. The cost of collection has been materially reduced; to such an extent that banks can afford to take country checks at par. The average time for collection has also been greatly reduced, with the result, among other advantages, of preventing the vicious practice resorted to by some weak banks of living largely upon the proceeds of collections for which they remit only after much delay. This method of handling country checks seems to have had something to do with the maintenance in New England of regular settlements between banks even during the crisis of 1907. Where such a mechanism is provided, insuring the steady and automatic presentation and payment of checks and drafts, there is much less likelihood that a bank will resort to delays and evasions as a means of strengthening itself in emergencies than under a regime which allows even in normal times more or less habitual delay.[1]

With our existing banks strengthened in ways such as were suggested in the two preceding articles, and with a central bank in position to insist upon the full use of their resources in handling emergencies, there would be little need of direct assistance from that institution. It should have sufficient lending power to give confidence in the stability of our banking system, but not the enormous strength which would be required if it were to be the entire support of our credit structure in periods of financial strain. In short, according to this plan the management of the central bank may be likened to the general staff of an army, while the bank itself in the exercise of its powers will be analogous to a reserve rather than an attacking force.

[1] On methods of clearing country checks see, in the National Monetary Commission Publications, J. G. Cannon, Clearing Houses, pp. 58–64, 259–276.

III

It does not come within the scope of this paper to present a detailed plan of organization for a central bank, still less to set forth the legislative restrictions upon its powers or the policy which should be followed by its management. These are matters which may be left for settlement if its primary functions are agreed to be of the kind which has been outlined. Attention will be directed in conclusion to a few matters of special importance or difficulty which should be kept in view in working out the details of a plan for a central bank.

Foreign experience shows very clearly that successful results have been achieved by central banks, differing widely one from another in the details of their organization. In the attainment of the objects in view from the establishment of such an institution, therefore, the determination of the most suitable form of organization for this country, while an occasion for constructive thought of a high order, is, after all, a matter of secondary importance. One thing, however, is essential. Much of the opposition to a central bank of any kind is based upon the fear that it might be controlled and used for selfish purposes by the powerful financial groups which control the large reserve-holding New York banks. This is not a very serious danger under any circumstances, because a central bank is made very nearly immune from such attempts by the publicity which attends its operations and even more by the constant public interest in its condition and policy. As a positive safeguard,

however, the form of organization can without difficulty be made such that the fears of the most dis-
trustful should be allayed. The management might
be made entirely independent of the shareholders,
as is the case with all central banks except the Bank
of England. A part of the directorate might well be
appointed by the federal government, tho perhaps
not the majority; and certainly not the entire board
as is the practice in most countries, the represen-
tatives of the shareholders having only an advisory
function. The national banks, organized into dis-
tricts for the purpose, might well be empowered to
choose some or even all of the directorate, quite regardless of whether the capital is to be subscribed by
them or not. Finally, if the capital is to be furnished
by individuals, the shareholders might have the power
to choose some number, less than a majority, of the
board. All three of these parties in interest might
share in determining the composition of the management of the bank. By any one of the means suggested
the likelihood of the bank being controlled for selfish
purposes, even for a short time, would be practically
nil and for any prolonged period an absolute impossibility.

There remains for consideration another safeguard
which would in large measure render valueless a successful attempt at gaining control. In Europe, central banks employ their funds mainly in discounts
or rediscounts of trade bills, tho they also make (invariably at a higher rate) a moderate amount of
advances upon collateral security. In emergencies
and especially in connection with arrangements for

the relief of particular banks, occasion for which
would be furnished by a situation such as that of
the New York trust companies in 1907, a central
bank in this country would find it necessary to make
advances upon collateral security. Ordinarily, however, it would probably be found advisable not to grant
any collateral loans. Such loans have altogether too
much vogue at present, our bankers greatly exag-
gerating their liquidness, at least in emergencies.
Even tho, in the development of the trade and industry of the country securities may be of as much
importance as the commercial bill, they are not so
satisfactory as a basis for bank loans. To a very
considerable extent collateral loans merely enable
weak holders to retain a large mass of securities which,
if held by persons able to pay for them outright,
would do much to strengthen our financial position.
No sound business depends upon bank loans for its
permanent capital requirements, but in so far as its
securities are held by means of such loans, an analogous situation is created. Of course, the restriction
of the business of the central bank to dealings in commercial paper would not prevent resort to it by banks
seeking additional funds to be used in collateral loans,
since all banks are certain to have some paper of the
commercial variety. But it would simplify matters
to a very considerable extent for the management,
and would also vastly diminish the utility of the bank
to any particular financial group and consequently
the temptation to seek a controlling voice in its management.

In recent discussion of the advantages which may be derived from a central bank much has been said of the desirability of domesticating the bank acceptance in this country.[1] It is urged that in its absence the loans of the banks are not and can not become truly liquid and also that through its use a loan market, as wide as the country, may be developed, so that all borrowers would secure the same rate upon a given grade of security. The proposal is attractive. But it is open to serious objections; and fortunately much of the advantage promised can be secured by other means involving far less danger.

If an acceptance will serve the requirements of a borrower he is far more likely to be accomodated by a bank than if it were necessary to grant him a loan. In both instances the bank incurs an obligation. In the case of the acceptance the obligation is entirely contingent upon the inability of the borrower to meet the bill when it matures. In the case of the loan the bank is subject to the same possibility of loss from the failure of the borrower to meet his obligations; but it has also the immediate obligation to supply him with the proceeds of the loan. The use of the bank acceptance involves a danger of excessive credit expansion which is most serious under our system of twenty thousand or more banks. Foreign example affords no indication whatever of what the results might be. In England, with its small number of banks of large average size, this business has been until recently carefully avoided, having been con-

---

[1] National Monetary Commission Publications; The Discount Market of Europe, by Paul M. Warburg; and Bank Acceptances, by L. M. Jacobs.

ducted entirely by a small number of accepting houses. On the Continent the acceptance has been in more general use, having been developed at first by private bankers, a very conservative class. Tho from the beginning of their history adopted by incorporated banks also, it must be remembered that the number of such institutions has never been large and that they have been generally of considerable size.

The bank acceptance would seem to be indispensable in connection with the financing of foreign trade; but for purely domestic trade its utility is relatively slight and its use seems to be generally declining. In our foreign trade it might readily be developed by foreign exchange banks, and this may be expected when rates for loans in this country decline to European levels so that it will be profitable to employ our capital for that purpose.

In purely domestic dealings the advantages promised from the use of the bank acceptance can be secured by other means involving far less risk of excessive credit expansion.[1] Even at present, many borrowers throughout the country secure through note brokers the lowest rates current on commercial loans. These rates, as well as those on commercial loans secured directly from the banks, are unreasonably high judged by foreign standards, inasmuch as they are higher than rates for collateral loans. If it may be assumed that banking profits are not excessive at present, it follows that all that can be expected through the

---

[1] It is probable that the bank acceptance would prove a safe and useful device if restricted to bills drawn by banks upon reserve agents; it might remove the unreasonable reluctance of many bankers to resort openly to advances from other banks when the legitimate local demand for loans exceeds their own resources.

adoption of any change in our credit machinery is a reversal of the relationship between these two classes of loans.[1] This will be accomplished through the central bank if its operations are confined to commercial paper. Indeed, it is the practice of lending at lower rates on trade bills than on collateral loans by the European central banks, rather than the bank acceptance, that gives the former its relatively low rate. Further, it is the preferential treatment of commercial paper which gives it its liquid character in foreign countries. The same policy followed by a central bank here will make the trade bill, whatever its form, a more liquid asset for the banks than the collateral loan and will consequently secure for it a more satisfactory rate.

Most of the plans for a central bank have agreed in assigning to it a capital of something like $100,000,000. But this amount would seem to be excessive for a bank of the kind here suggested. A capital of $50,000,000 would be considerably greater than that of any other central bank except that of the Bank of England, whose capital is entirely tied up in the government debt. Dividends upon the shares of the bank should be limited either to a fixed maximum or by turning over to the government a progressively increasing proportion of profits. Even with profits

[1] European bankers might employ temporarily idle funds in our commercial bill market if the bank acceptance were adopted, but the amount of such funds would probably not be large enough to affect appreciably the rate for loans. The wide fluctuations in foreign exchange rates between markets separated by wide distances would be an obstacle. Moreover, it would be extremely hazardous to become dependent upon large amounts of so fluctuating a resource. It is not a serious matter in London because in addition to its own domestic and foreign trade the foreign trade of other countries is also largely financed there.

limited in this way, however, a large capital invites
the danger of an unnecessary extension of the operations of the bank in order to earn a moderate return
to shareholders.

Experience shows very conclusively that it is unwise
to hamper a central bank with restrictions upon the
extent to which it may extend its credits either in the
form of notes or deposits. Presumably a central
bank in this country would find it desirable to maintain in normal times a specie reserve of at least 50
per cent against its demand liabilities, but it should
feel no hesitation in, and certainly should not be prevented by law from, going as far below that proportion
as might be necessary in handling emergencies. But
legislative provisions, which without limiting the
possible amount would impede somewhat the issue
of its notes, might serve the useful purpose of shielding
the bank from unreasonable demands for accomodation. No advantage is to be gained through an
increase in the amount of paper substitutes for coin
so long as the present undesirably large increase in
the gold supply of the world continues. Both monetary and banking requirements would seem to be best
served by granting the bank the right, free from
taxation, to issue an amount of notes equal to
its gold holdings, while all additional issues upon
which there would be no definite limit might be subject to a tax of at least 5 per cent. The issue of
taxable notes need not be regarded as in any way an
emergency measure. The tax would restrain the
management somewhat but its primary purpose
would be to shelter the Bank from the criticism of

over-sanguine citizens unable to perceive in periods of active business the wisdom of a refusal to extend credit to the extreme limits of safety.

In addition to the funds subscribed by its shareholders the Bank would also secure funds deposited by the other banks to enable them to make use of its exchange and clearing service, and also the funds constituting the working balance of the United States Treasury. It might, too, secure a still further accession of funds, and at the same time relieve the government of a portion of its monetary burdens, if the issue of gold certificates were discontinued and the present certificates redeemed. On account of the preference of the people for paper money much of the gold thus paid out would certainly be taken to the central bank to be exchanged for its notes. This gold would largely augment the general banking reserve of the Bank since it would not be held as a special deposit against the notes.[1] At the same time the $346,000,000 of greenbacks might also be exchanged for the notes of the Bank, the $150,000,000 gold reserve being turned into its general reserve. As a result of these arrangements two kinds of money now in general use would disappear from circulation, the gold certificate and the United States note, and would be replaced by the notes of the central bank. The government would cease to be responsible for any kind of paper except the silver certificates. The amount of these, however,

---

[1] Much of the strength of the Bank of France is to be attributed to this preference for paper money. The stock of money in circulation has increased in France with the growth of population and business, and on account of the increase in the world's supply of gold. This gold, instead of going directly into circulation, has been largely taken to the Bank of France to be exchanged for bank-notes.

is far less than is always required for monetary purposes outside the banks and they no longer present a serious monetary problem. They might, indeed, be taken over by the bank in exchange for its notes. The reserve of the bank would then be composed in part of silver; but in this respect it would not be unlike some very successful central banks, notably those of France and Germany. At the outset, however, it might well prove the wiser policy not to weaken the prestige of the bank in this way. By reserving for the silver certificate the one-dollar and two-dollar denominations, and by restricting the volume of bank-notes of the next two denominations, sufficient use would be provided for the existing volume of silver certificates, the position of which would then be somewhat analogous to that of subsidiary coin.

The outcome of these monetary changes will be made somewhat more evident by the construction of a statement of the condition of the Bank just before opening its doors for business. Most of its liabilities can be stated with some certainty: viz. capital $50,-000,000; U. S. notes $346,000,000; U. S. Treasury account (taking its present condition as a basis) $160,000,000,[1] and, finally, the deposits of bankers for clearing and exchange purposes, which may be estimated at $75,000,000. The assets of the Bank can be estimated less exactly, because of the impossibility of knowing the proportion of the different kinds of money now in circulation which would be turned into the Bank. Subscription to its capital

[1] I have not included in this statement the item of $36,000,000 of U. S. deposits now held by the national banks. Presumably, much of this amount would be transferred to the central bank, tho perhaps not at the outset.

might reasonably be made payable in gold or gold
certificates. Upon assuming responsibility for U. S.
notes, the Bank would receive the $150,000,000 gold
reserve. The remaining $196,000,000 might perhaps
be taken care of by assigning a government debt to
the Bank which, as in the case of the Bank of England,
would be a book debt not subject to sale. This obligation need not involve any interest charge on the
government. Even if interest were paid, it would
be a matter of no special importance, in view of the
limitation of dividend to be paid to shareholders.
The Treasury balance would give the Bank $95,000,-
000 in gold and $65,000,000 in other kinds of money
made up as follows: $5,000,000 in U. S. notes, about
$30,000,000 in bank-notes, and a similar amount in
silver and subsidiary coin. Assuming that the deposits of the Bank would be made up of $50,000,000
in gold and $25,000,000 in U. S. notes; and cancelling
the $30,000,000 of U. S. notes, the statement of con-
dition of the Bank would be as follows: —

Liabilities		Resources	
Capital .	. . . $50,000,000	Gov't debt	$196,000,000
U.S. notes	. . . 316,000,000	Gold	325,000,000
U.S. Treas. account	160,000,000	Silver	30,000,000
Due to other banks .	75,000,000	Notes of other banks	30,000,000
	$601,000,000		$601,000,000

The Bank would have a gold reserve of more than
62 per cent of its demand liabilities. Its power to
issue notes, however, before reaching the taxable
limit would be slight, only $29,000,000. But that
would be an advantage from the point of view which

has been emphasized in this article. In normal times the rediscounts made by the Bank would probably involve an increase mainly in its deposit liabilities rather than in the volume of its notes in circulation. Restricted to dealings with other banks there is some doubt whether sufficient business would be regularly secured to enable the Bank to meet expenses and provide a moderate dividend on its shares.[1] Much might be said in favor of a government guaranty of three per cent on the $50,000,000 of capital. It would be a small price to pay the Bank for taking over U. S. notes and for handling the receipts and disbursements of the government.

The extent and the rapidity with which the gold holdings of the Bank would be increased through the exchange of gold for its notes can not be even roughly estimated. It would seem probable that many banks would prefer to hold gold or gold certificates in their reserves rather than the notes of the Bank. On the other hand, gold certificates received in payments to it would be cancelled and either gold or notes paid out according to the preference of customers. Moreover, a considerable portion of future additions to the gold supply would probably be exchanged for notes on account of the preference of the people for a paper circulating medium. This exchange of gold for notes would not increase the power of the Bank to issue untaxed notes but would greatly strengthen its reserve and consequently its ability to extend its operations and to meet any strain upon its resources.

[1] Idle funds might be employed profitably in the purchase and holding until maturity of foreign commercial bills of exchange. There could be no opposition by the other banks on the ground of competition.

This growth would, in part, be paralleled by that in the number and volume of business of the other banks. Even if ultimately the Bank should attract to itself the means for extending the scope of its operations, that need not be a ground for apprehension. At the outset it would be most important that the Bank should not be overburdened with responsibilities and that the other banks should not rely upon it as the sole support of the credit structure. But when experience had shown that the other banks continued to maintain themselves in a condition of reasonable strength, and that the central bank could secure the use of their resources in emergencies, it might then with safety engage in operations which would have been extremely hazardous at the beginning of its activities.

www.ingramcontent.com/pod-product-compliance
Lightning Source LLC
Chambersburg PA
CBHW070649290526
45790CB00001B/245